WORDS ON THE TABLE

OTHER COLLECTIONS OF POETRY IN ENGLISH
FROM COLENSO BOOKS

Sweet-voiced Sappho: some of the extant poems of Sappho of Lesbos and other Ancient Greek poets translated into English verse by Theodore Stephanides (2015)

The fruitful discontent of the word: a further collection of poems by Lawrence Durrell, edited by Peter Baldwin (2018)
(a supplement to Durrell's *Collected Poems 1931–1974*
Faber and Faber, London, 1985)

Yannis Ritsos among his contemporaries: twentieth-century Greek poetry, translated by Marjorie Chambers (2018)

The Golden Face by Theodore Stephanides, 2nd edition
(1st edition 1965, The Fortune Press, London)
with facing Greek translation by Vera Konidari (2019)

Reading the signs
by Jim Potts (2020)

Viral Verse: pandemic poems and images
by sixteen contributors (2020)

Memorials, nightscapes, etcetera: poems of several decades
by Anthony Hirst (2020)

POEMS BY JIM POTTS HAVE APPEARED IN THE FOLLOWING PUBLICATIONS:

Spectator (London: English Department, London University Institute of Education, 1966); see also page 2.

Two point five edited by Tom Corbett, Victor French and Simon Heywood (London: The Poetry Society, London University Institute of Education, 1967).

16 Poems/16 Básní by Jim Potts, bilingual edition with Czech translations by Ladislav Verecký, Pavel Šrut and Ivo Šmoldas (Prague: Koháček & Trnka, 1989).

The Haiku Hundred edited by James Kirkup, David Cobb and Peter Mortimer (North Shields: Iron Press, 1992).

Swedish Reflections, from Beowulf to Bergman, edited by Judith Black and Jim Potts (London: Arcadia Books, 2003).

Corfu Blues by Jim Potts (Stockholm: Ars Interpres Publications, 2006).

The Cat of Portovecchio: Corfu Tales by Maria Strani-Potts (Blackheath NSW: Brandl and Schlesinger, 2007).

The Haiku 100 edited by Peter Mortimer, The Historic Collection (North Shields: Iron Press, 2015).

Reading the signs by Jim Potts (London: Colenso Books 2020).

AND ALSO IN THE FOLLOWING PERIODICALS:

Ars Intrepres: International Journal of Poetry, Translation and Art; Acumen; Cadences; and the *William Barnes Society Newsletter.*

AND IN TRANSLATION IN:

Porphyras, Odos Panos, Endefktirio, Tomes, Ipeirotika Grammata and *O Phileleftheros* (Greek); *Calende: Revistă de cultură* (Romanian); *Lyrikvännen* (Swedish); and *Minimanimalia: Canzoniere Animinimalista di Raul Scacchi*, ed. Gioia R. Maestro Scacchi (Italian).

OTHER BOOKS BY JIM POTTS

The Ionian Islands and Epirus: A Cultural History (Oxford: Signal Books; New York: Oxford University Press; 2010).

This Spinning World: 43 Stories from far and wide (London: Colenso Books, 2019).

WORDS ON THE TABLE

POEMS BY JIM POTTS

COLENSO BOOKS
2021

This collection first published October 2021 by
Colenso Books
68 Palatine Road, London N16 8ST, UK
colensobooks@gmail.com

ISBN 978-1-912788-21-7

Copyright © 2021 Jim Potts

"Create!" and "Party piece" were first published in *Spectator* (1966); "Create!" was republished in *16 poems* (1989)

"The only problem" was first published (as "Il n'y a qu'un problème") in *Two point five* (1967).

"Podpis" was first published in *Acumen* 4 (October 1986).

"Memories of Asia Minor", "Dampier's landfalls in New Holland", "The dream that came true — Captain Cook at Kealakekua Bay", "Ordained by Fate (and Yalta)" and "Semiotics — Marrickville" (as "Multicultural Semiotics: Marrickville") were first published in *Ars Interpres* 4–5 (October 2005); the first one and the last two were republished in *Corfu Blues* (2006)

"You are my cathedral", "The artist", "Costa's curse", "Smrt", "The killer", "The Apocalyptic Blues", "First impressions of Prague", "To the Czechs" and "Arbeit macht frei" were first published in *16 Poems* (1989); "The artist" and "Costa's curse" were republished in *Corfu Blues* (2006).

"Either/Or", "Parking place", "Confessions of an unconfirmed man", "Mandoukiotissa", "Bosnia, November 1991", "Paxiot fisherman", "Polite/aggressive", "Kerkyra", "A nice guy — don't get me wrong", "War Zone, Ionian Sea", "Corcyra/Dodona", "Xenitia", "With Ryōkan in a mountain hut in Epirus", "After Roy Acuff", "Our ethnic neighbours", "In praise of Bataria, the fiddler of Romiosyni", "Blues limerick", "Ali Pasha, Tepelenë", "Na ta poume?", "In the Good Old Days of Metaxas", "Zagori", "Corfu blues (song)", "Iannis Xenakis", "Greek music", "Bellou's Birthday Burial, 29 August 1997", "Gaida man", "A hermit in Vitsa", "Byron haiku", "Enver Hodja on Lord Byron (1975)", "Corfu", "One more spring", "Whatever Seferis says", "Alexander the Great", "Ouranoupolis — the border with Mount Athos", "Border guard", "Land of Albania!", "The revolution's not over", "Neo Frourio, Kerkyra", "Lazaretto", "Return — the collapse of the Greek–Italian Front after the intervention of Germany", "Welcome", "Nikolaides", "Martial Law (marching song)", "Paidomazomo, Prague Airport, 1988", "Stavrula's father" and "Black Sea — decomposition — searching for loved ones at Kerch, Spring 1942" were first published in *Corfu Blues* (2006).

"2013, the sky, maybe" was first published in *Cadences* 9 (2013).

"Mother and son — Beaminster", "Folk songs", "Before I come to Came" and "On a marble bust of Thomas Hardy" were first published in the *William Barnes Society Newsletter* 81 (Autumn 2020)

For publication details of books and pamphlets referred to above, see the page facing the title page.

The other 136 poems in this collection appear here for the first time in print, though a few have been featured on websites.

CONTENTS

DEDICATION	xiii
IN MEMORY OF	xv
INTRODUCTION	xvii
ACKNOWLEDGEMENTS	xxiii

Birth, life, death	1
C V	3
An alabaster jar for my mother	4
Führer	4
Dig that!	5
Working for Billy Butlin, Summer 1963	6
In the kindergarten night	7
Palma euphoria	8
Our elastic love	8
Either/Or	9
Dagmar	9
Kyria Elena	9
You are my cathedral	10
Mother and son — Beaminster	10
Easter Sunday, Sherborne Abbey	11
Create!	12
Party piece	12
The artist	14
Costa's curse	15
Parking place	15
Moving house, from Somerset to Dorset	16
Confession of an unconfirmed man	17
Mandoukiotissa	17
Athens, nefos and seismos, 1982	18
Tbilisi toast-master	18
Dawn chorus, Sherborne, for Nina-Maria	19
Fathers v. Sons	20
West Saxon Nap	20

Abe and Mary	21
Bosnia, November 1991	21
Helsinki, November 2000	22
Plain sailing	22
Paxiot fisherman	22
On the ferry from Finnhamn	22
Covering the war in Afghanistan	23
For Jack, two days old	24
"I'm glad I'm not a Baghdad grandad"	24
Stockholm Sunday	25
The Incident Hot-Line, September 2003	25
Performance art (Stockholm)	26
Helsinki, Friday 13 June 2003	26
Paranoid at fifty-nine	27
Polite/aggressive on Flight OA601, Corfu–Athens	28
Thirty words of my first grandson	29
Kerkyra	30
New York	31
Rostock, November 2004	31
A nice guy — don't get me wrong	32
Foxy Lady (Neo-Nazi)	32
Breakfast at The Royal Oak	33
Three score and ten	33
Good augury	34
The only problem / Le seul problème	34
The sea	35
War Zone, Ionian Sea	35
In Oslo	36
Before I come to Came	36
Life is short	37
Brain damage	37
Corcyra/Dodona	38
Smrt	38
První Máj (Mayday)	38
The Devil's Advocate and the Coronavirus Pandemic	39
"Bella"	39
Podpis	40
On the need to study longer with Professor Yu Qilong	40

Hamilton haiku for a clever QC	41
Xenitia	41
Bashō, 1644	42
Bashō's bones	42
With Ryōkan in a mountain hut in Epirus	42
Grim prospects — autumnal Monday	43
Sani, Halkidiki	43
Potsherds and middens	44
Physics and philosophy	44
Brave cowards	45
Christmas	45
The bench	45

Songs and singers 47

Musical education	49
Haydn's wife	49
Bohemian folk song (Volksweise)	50
Folk songs	50
Žert, 1986	52
The guitar	52
After Roy Acuff	53
Song of the young hobo	53
Blues Pilgrimage	54
The Original Dixieland Jazz Band (Billy Jones, piano)	56
"A red house over yonder"	56
The Killer	57
All hail, Mrs Clinkscales! Echoes of Ellington, Washington, DC	58
Elvis Lenin	59
Carrying the torch for Billie	60
The late Howlin' Wolf and the World Information Order	60
Swedish Schnapps	61
Johnny Ace, RIP, 25 December 1954	61
The Nomad	62
Masenko — Ethiopian single-horsehair-stringed bowed lute	63
Eskista	64
A, ai ge (Sad song at Simatai)	64
The singer who defected	65

The Apocalyptic Blues	66
"Our ethnic neighbours"	67
The Fall of the Wall — Begrüßungsgeld (welcome money)	68
In praise of Bataria, the fiddler of Romiosyni	69
Blues limerick	69
Ali Pasha, Tepelenë	69
"Na ta poume?"	70
Memories of Asia Minor — improvisation in a minor key	71
In the Good Old Days of Metaxas	72
Zagori	73
Corfu Blues (song)	74
Iannis Xenakis	75
Greek music	76
Bellou's Birthday Burial, 29 August 1997	76
Gaida man	77
Easter 1966 (song)	78

The written word 79

Code of practice	81
A hermit in Vitsa	81
Lizzy Siddal, model and muse, artist and poet	82
The humanists' raffle	83
LEL — on an entry in the Dictionary of National Biography	84
Skeletons of the past — a drunken man on Burns Night, 1959	84
Byron haiku	85
Enver Hoxha on Lord Byron (1975)	86
Racedown, Dorset, September 1795 – June 1797	86
Jack Kerouac	87
Big Sur to Bodega Bay — Jack Kerouac and Henry Miller haunt the Big Sur cabins	88
The Beats abroad	89
The character of D. K. Toteras	90
2013, the sky, maybe	91
Corfu	91
One more spring	92
Whatever Seferis says	93

Josef Jungmann's Paradise Lost (Ztracený Ráj, 1811) —	
riot police by the statue of Jungmann	93
November cloud	94
Kafka and Steiner, Prague, 28 March 1911	96
Rilke at Duino, Joyce at Trieste	96
Die Spätbürgerliche Lyrik	97
Albert Camus visits Prague, 1936	97
In memory of Georgi Ivanov Markov	98
Yang's comparison — ancient and modern	98
To some British poets leaving Prague	99
The Danube — on Ister Bank	100
A Doll's House for Germany	100
Auden and Dresden	101
Paul Potts (1911–1990)	102
The Little Nobel	103
Sharp poem	103
Sirmione, Lake Garda	104
Calligrapher	104

Facing off the Thought Police 105

Thoughtcrimes	107
On a marble bust of Thomas Hardy, 1915–2015	107
Dampier's landfalls in New Holland	108
Wogganmagule	109
Red Hands Cave	110
The dream came true — Captain Cook at Kealakekua Bay	110
Diamantina Roma and the postings of Governor Bowen	112
At Salamanca Market, Hobart	113
Imagined last words	114
Port Arthur — Isle of the Dead	114
Reflecting, unreflecting	116
Semiotics — Marrickville	116
Diplomatic Claptrap Rap	117
Suburban Backlash — Islamophobia	118
Pyrotechnics, November 5th	118
Venice	119
The Good Life	119

Sankt Göran och draken	120
Alexander the Great	120
The Stockholm Syndrome ("The party has just begun")	121
Retired Torturers	121
Paranoia — risk för istappar!	122
Paxos	122
Portland tipping bridge — the feuding fisherman who trespassed on quarrymen's land	123
The Igoumenos and the Saint	123
Ouranoupolis — the border with Mount Athos	123
Acheiropoieta	124
On the need for a new Mission	124
Border guard	124
Land of Albania!	125
The revolution's not over	126
Neo Frourio, Kerkyra	127
Lazaretto	127
Along came Luccheni	127
Return — the collapse of the Greek–Italian Front after the intervention of Germany	128
Pylos	128
Ordained by Fate (and Yalta)	129
Welcome	129
Nikolaides	130
Martial Law (marching song)	131
Paidomazomo, Prague Airport, 1988	132
Stavrula's father	132
Hack! The Totalitarian Party poet and the 1952 Show Trials	134
The Red Danube, near Devín Castle, Bratislava	134
First impressions of Prague	136
Right of way — "All in Bohemia's well"	136
The giants	137
Karel Čapek and Mr Esquire, music reporter of *The Times*, 1938	138
Karel Čapek's dying words?	139
To the Czechs	139
Jan Palach	140
Václav Havel's Trial	140

Black Sea — decomposition — searching for loved ones at Kerch, Spring 1942	141
On the Silesian Express to Warsaw	142
Arbeit macht frei	143
Last Christmas in Prague — Kaprová Koleda	143
Persons of Interest	144
POSTSCRIPT ON CZECHOSLOVAKIA	145
NOTES	151

DEDICATION

To all the members of my family
Maria Potts (Maria Strani-Potts)
Nina-Maria Potts
Alexander Potts
Roy Potts
David Rennie
Priscillia Robineau
and my five grandchildren, Jack, Ella, Théo, Milo and Eva

To the friends in many countries (I regret there is not space to name them all here) who have kindly taken an interest in my literary endeavours over the years, and especially to

Mark Charles Allen
Anthony Hirst
Demetris Dallas
Ian Whitwham
Dimitris Konidaris
Demosthenes Kalakos
Maria Pouliasi
Fantina Kardaki
Lena Koronaki
Alexander Deriev
Ivo Šmoldas
Kyoko Ando
Christopher C. King
Bronwen Katsaros
Linda Fagioli-Katsiotas
Henry Denander
Annabelle Louvros
Flavio Andreis
Rea Ann-Margaret Mellberg
Ekaterini Douka-Kabitoglou
Tasoula Pechlivanos
Julian Nangle
Michael Rosen

IN MEMORY OF

Nina Kathleen and James Kenneth Potts, *my mother and father*
B. D. Baker, *my maternal grandmother*
Sally Potts, *my paternal grandmother*

*and of poets, other writers and composers with whom
I have corresponded or exchanged ideas in the past:*

Jimmie Katsaros
Demetrius Toteras
Raul Scacchi
Adrian Mitchell
Dannie Abse
Glyn Hughes
Alan Sillitoe
Dimitris Tsaloumas
Dimitris Doukaris
Niki Marangou
Miroslav Holub
Ewald Osers
Faysal Mikdadi
Pavel Šrut
Ladislav Verecký
Ian Templeman
Izzy Young
Jozef Blaho
Yannis Ritsos
Erotokritos Moraitis
John Lee Hooker
Mikis Theodorakis

INTRODUCTION

Putting words on the table is a little like laying one's cards on the table. Writing and sharing poems has been a risky business in a number of countries at certain periods. Freedom of speech is a recurrent theme in these poems.

Some of my poems may seem too pointed or unguarded for a "non-political" person living and working in countries which exercised strict censorship and harassed writers, translators and dissidents at various times. If diplomacy involves tact, circumspection, discretion and respect for etiquette, this collection of poems is not always as diplomatic or tactful as I attempted to be during my working life in countries as varied as Ethiopia, Kenya, Greece, Czechoslovakia, Australia and Sweden.

My personal mission has always been to build bridges between people, to foster friendship and mutual understanding, closer contact between writers, musicians, artists, academics and scientists.

> Dear Jim,
>
> I read your and Maria's interviews in Friendship Magazine. They are both excellent. It is not bad to hear that the city of Prague is a pleasant place for you. But what's more: our children from Šumava to Tatras will read your open words about barbed-wire and freedom of expression. That's just what they need.

I once received the above letter from "Pavel", probably a teacher in Slovakia. His surname was not on the letter, which was dated the 19th of June 1989, five months before the non-violent or "velvet" revolution in Czechoslovakia, the fall of the communist government and the fall of the Berlin Wall. He referred to an interview I had given to a magazine called *L'Amitié / Friendship*, aimed at Czech and Slovak learners of the English and French languages; it was distributed to all secondary schools throughout the country:

"Our children, from Šumava to Tatras, will read your open words about barbed-wire and freedom of expression. That's just what they need."

He wasn't being ironical.

Do you have any wishes for the future?

Apart from a Europe without frontiers, or at least without barbed-wire, my wishes for the future would certainly include greater tolerance and understanding in the world, less fanaticism and terrorism, more respect for human rights everywhere, and a united attack on environmental pollution, whether in the streets of London or of Prague, and cleaner rivers and seas. Since my next job is going to be concerned with Literature, I would say that freedom of expression is the most important issue. I would wish to see more people stand up for that idea.

In *Words on the table* I now reclaim some freedom for myself. The collection stands beside *Reading the signs* and *This spinning world* as a further contribution to the cause. Some of the poems are testimonies to the times, to the thoughts and experiences I have had in different countries, "facing off the thought police" (if only in my private journals or inside my own head).

In several countries where I have lived and worked — especially in totalitarian states which at times practised strict censorship — poetry, like music, has proved necessary for survival and mental health.

"Facing off the thought police" has been, however, only part of my story and many of the poems in this book come from periods long before my travels began. The earliest, written when I was fifteen or sixteen, was my first samizdat poem, distributed to a few friends — it wouldn't have been considered suitable for the school magazine.

> FÜHRER
>
> Hypocritical political
> Leaders. Breeders
> Of contempt, exempt
> From humanity;
> Filled with insane
> And empty vanity.
> Only seeking in reality,
> Power, fame and private gain.

Some years before I went to university, I discovered the healing powers of the real, deep blues, in part as a means to confront and overcome our stressful sense of the Absurd.

In my article, "Blues and the Absurd", published in *Isis*, an Oxford student publication,[1] I quoted from a blues album sleeve note by Jacques Demêtre, the French blues and gospel music historian:

> The blues was able to conjure up and to dispel the moods which described it. It held the promise of liberty.

I also wrote of Antoine Roquentin, Sartre's protagonist in the novel *La Nausée* whose sense of existential nausea was dispelled on listening to an old ragtime jazz-blues, "Some of these days, you'll miss me honey!"

James Baldwin wrote of the "ironic tenacity" of many blues singers. Albert Camus might have called singing the blues — or the writing of a poem — an act of rebellion against the Absurd.

I call to mind some words by Jack London from *The Star*

[1] *Isis* 1472, week ending 17 October 1964.

Rover, which echo Blakes' sentiments in *Songs of Experience*:

> Ah, truly, shades of the prison-house close about us, the
> new-born things, and all too soon do we forget.

I wish I could have attained the profoundly expressive poetic directness of the songs of a folk-blues *homme révolté* like Charley (sometimes "Charlie") Patton. For me, his version of the "Some of these days" theme is the most powerful. And I wish I could have achieved something of the healing effect of an Epirot klarino player consoling a whole village community with a moving lament (*miroloyi*), or an Aboriginal didgeridoo player healing members of his traditional tribal community.

In 1967, a year after I graduated, I was greatly encouraged by a long letter from Adrian Mitchell, to whom I'd sent a collection of my poems called *Word-Salad*, a title that was possibly influenced by my reading of some works of R. D. Laing.[2] Writing from Bentham, Lancaster, as a Fellow in the Arts at the University of Lancaster, Adrian gave me helpful comments on most of the poems and song lyrics, telling me which poems he liked best and which poems he wanted to hear set to music and sung. "Dear Jim," he wrote, "thank you for letting me see Word-Salad, which excites me." In the end I did nothing with the collection as such,[3] because I went to live on a Greek island, where I had accepted a teaching post (or "dropped out" temporarily), but Adrian's letter meant a lot to me, as did his own collection *Out Loud*, and his lively poetry performances.

The title *Word-Salad* would not in any case have been appropriate, given that it is a psychiatric (or anti-Psychiatry) term relating to the realm of schizophrenia and the "divided self". The term still strikes me as more generally useful. If this collection is not in any sense a "word-salad", perhaps it resembles a mixed salad (what some used to call, equally inappropriately, a *macédoine*), a mixture or medley of things with a lot of diversity and variety.

---

[2] R. D. Laing (1927–1989) was a controversial psychotherapist and influential thinker (now less fashionable), author of many books including *The Divided Self* (1960) and *The Politics of Experience and the Bird of Paradise* (1967).

[3] Most of the pre-1968 poems and songs, however, appear here or in *Reading the signs* and/or in *Corfu Blues*.

My unpublished 1960's collection, *Word-Salad*, carried a quotation (which still resonates for me), from Laing's *The Politics of Experience*:

> Words in a poem, sounds in movement, rhythm in space, attempt to capture personal meaning in personal time and space from out of the sights and sounds of a depersonalized, dehumanized world. They are bridgeheads into alien territory. They are acts of insurrection. Their source is from the Silence at the centre of each of us

For many years I had also planned to publish a collection to be called *World Music*, which would have included all the poems in the second section of this book, "Songs and singers" and some others, but I am pleased that I saved them for this more comprehensive and representative volume.

I hope the collection does not come across as a "word-salad" in the psychiatric sense — confused, disordered, disorganised, random or unintelligible. I have my editor, the poet Anthony Hirst, to thank for helping me avoid that outcome.

If some of my poems fail to appeal to, or to heal others, they have, like the blues, at least helped to keep *me* feeling both free and sane! So here they are, my words, face-up on the table.

Jim Potts, Dorchester
April 4th, 2021

ACKNOWLEDGEMENTS

The last two years have been bad for most human beings, but good for poetry. International travel has been largely out of the question, so I have had to revisit my favourite countries in my dreams, by reading about them or by revisiting significant places through memories evoked during the collection and revision of these poems. Looking back, I would like to thank and acknowledge the following:

Anthony Hirst, for his craftsmanship, care and creativity as editor and publisher, and for sharing his own poetry before and after the lockdowns.

Alexander Deriev, formerly publisher of Ars Interpres and my book *Corfu Blues*, and of the international journal, *Ars Interpres*.

The William Barnes Society, and in particular Alan Chedzoy, the editor of the Society's *Newsletter*, and Brian Caddy, Mark North, and the much-missed Marion Tait, editors of the Society's website.

My past translators, and especially Demetris Dallas who is still working on his extensive Greek translations of my poems.

Ivo Šmoldas, the only survivor of the three Czech translators of my poems in *16 Poems*.

Julian Nangle, poet and host of the convivial Open Mic Poetry Readings at his bookshop, Books Beyond Words (now closed) in Dorchester, where some of these poems were first given an airing.

The late Raul Scacchi, a friend and project collaborator who set and arranged some of my poems and lyrics, and whose own song compositions and concept albums still move me.

Mark Allen, publisher, my oldest friend, author of the novel *Life Term*, for sharing his own writings and for his enduring optimism throughout the pandemic.

Maria, Nina-Maria and Alex, for their continuing support in all things.

Birth,

life,

death

"An alabaster jar for my mother" (page 4)

Cover of a cyclostyled collection of prose and poetry (1966) by postgraduate students in the English Department of the Institute of Education, University of London, in which the poems "Create!" and "Party piece" (pages 12–13) first appeared

CV

Between V-2 and Atom Bomb
I was born. Halfway between D-Day
and Hiroshima. Born British, in Bristol,
winter, 1944.
Far away in Chicago
Big Joe Turner and boogie-woogie Pete
were playing and singing the night away
the very day I saw the light.
"I ain't had no real good lovin' . . ."
As a baby, I had good loving.
A few short months before Yalta
I let out my first yell.
I kept on yelling.
Perhaps I could hear the bombs hit Dresden,
perhaps I already knew
half of Europe was lost.
I'm glad at least I couldn't see
the opening of the Death Camps,
the British Liberation troops
in Constitution Square;
the Americans at ease in Pilsen,
the Russian troops approaching Prague.

An alabaster jar for my mother

The delicate alabaster jar,
of palest pink, blue-veined,
which I, a humble schoolboy sculptor
carved for you (the jar you keep your pearls in),
remains, after thirty years, my proudest creation,
more precious than any marble masterpiece,
more gracious, in my memory, than any Grecian urn:
fragile, like my feelings, gently filed and chiselled,
sanded and polished to a blushing finish,
breast-smooth; of palest pink, blue-veined.

Führer
(my first "samizdat" poem, at age 15 or 16)

Hypocritical political
leaders. Breeders
of contempt, exempt
from humanity;
filled with insane
and empty vanity.
Only seeking in reality
power, fame and private gain.

Dig that!

I was Americanized early.
Though I was always last one in to bat,
I opened the bowling.
As a fielder
I had no peer.
I could hurl the ball from the boundary line
and hit the wicket with such a deadly aim
that the stumps would go flying, they'd be run out—
we'd shout "Howzat!"
in deepest rural Somerset.
When I was only twelve,
I'd won my colours, my First Eleven cap.
But I offended the Head,
he hauled me over the mat,
when I hollered in triumph,
"DIG THAT!"
"Dig that?"
It wasn't cricket —
so he used the bat.
Dig that.
The first rebellion
of a real cool cat.

Working for Billy Butlin, Summer 1963

I was working in the kitchens down at Butlin's in Minehead, a holiday job, to save money to hitch-hike abroad before going to university. My job? Washer of dishes-cum-kitchen-porter, alongside friendly seasonal drifters, there for fun and sex and a fiver a week.

Giant machines for washing dishes, the conveyor belts undermanned, only half the required crew to load, unload and load again. Machines to swallow thirty thousand dishes after every foul and fatty meal; plates stacked up high and stuck together, egg-yolks congealed like epoxy-glue. They're scoured by fast-revolving brushes, but still they come out yellow. Rough detergent and red-hot plates cause dermatitis on our hands. No gloves supplied.

Ten hours a day, the work's never finished; we're forbidden to leave before it's done. Breakfast, lunch and supper too. Norwegian students and grateful Czechs are here to improve their English.

We stagger out to a second job, just to earn a living wage, waiters in Billy's music-hall. If we spill a drink we pay for it. Foreign students feel conned, exploited; thought they'd come to our coast on a "working hol" — more like hard, forced-labour hell. No one's allowed to join a union, ever, or to leave the job, until at least a month is over (all wages earned can be withheld). Minimum contract period "five weeks".

The Department of Health may close the camp, it's rumoured; one of my chalet mates claims the VD rate's beyond control. The kitchen floor's inch-deep in dirt, fallen food's picked up to be re-plated . . . all those sticky, greasy plates . . . *recurrent nightmares, let me not forget* . . .

Billy was knighted in '64.

In the kindergarten night
(Wadham College, Oxford, 1964)

In the kindergarten night
when every letter
seems a runic symbol, a shape
without a corresponding sound —
fricative, explosive,
or guttural,
as in the garden of the world;
in the kindergarten night
when the children have not yet learned to dance
round Maypole or Forbidden Tree,
nor to chant in unison
both the War Cry and the Creed;
in the kindergarten night
we learn to place the lettered play-bricks
one upon the other
until the towers, too tall, collapse,
topple over in confusion
into our unsuspecting laps.

In the kindergarten night
we spell out with the letters of innocence
some primeval runic curse.

Palma euphoria
(Majorca, 1964)

Above the moon at midnight
no man so tall so soon.
I stretch out my arms —
what wingspan!
There's an albatross within me —
somewhere down there is the man.

Our elastic love
(Casablanca, 1964)

Our elastic love
wraps round
the waist
of the world.
It stretches
in any direction
and always remains
secure and fast.
This love of ours
will last;
for it is tied
to the future,
as well as
to the past.

Either / Or

Man of Letters or Man of Leisure,
which is it to be?
Wait and see.

Dagmar
(Jesolo, Venice, Summer 1965)

Day-bright
day-bright diamond
day-bright diamond of the hour-glass sands.

Kyria Elena

A relatively rational old Greek lady
claimed her plasma TV screen
followed every move she made.
She didn't suffer from dementia,
paranoia was not her scene,
but she'd keep shouting, "Turn it off!"
Or she'd cover it quickly with a cloth.
She didn't want the starving people
to watch her eating like some bourgeois toff.

You are my cathedral
(Cologne, September, 1965)

In the greystone glacial stillness
perpendiculars bend and pray . . .

Gothic fingers forged with grace
clasp together and coldly grasp
the pride from all but me.

Though the organ invades the inner void,
rolls loud with its cold acoustics,
not God, not Bach can make me buckle,
and yet I nearly kneel.

In the music you echo on,
overpowering all.
You are my cathedral.

Mother and son — Beaminster

Noo bigger pleace, noo gaÿer town,
Beyond thy sweet bells' dyèn soun',
As they do ring, or strike the hour . . .
William Barnes, "Be'mi'ster"

The Beaminster church bells
called us to listen:
compelled by the bells
we parked there and hearkened:
so much ringing of changes,
such chiming in tune.

Easter Sunday, Sherborne Abbey

I lost my camera
in Sherborne Abbey,
right at the start of Matins.
We'd shifted our pew
for a better view —
but then I couldn't focus.

Hymns and psalms,
the preacher, prayers,
readings from the Bible:
they passed me by,
(canon's voice too high?)
I really wasn't with it.

Christ Has Risen,
but my camera's missing,
I'm ill at ease in Sherborne Abbey.

Retrieved, relieved,
once the service ended.
That was a kind of blessing.

Create!
(London, 1966)

Labouring to synthesize
the perfect oval eggshell
we feel we must despise
our gifts, until we've been through hell.
"Touch me with noble anguish
make me suffer, damn you,
can't you see? —
warmth and human kindness
never weaned a genius-to-be."

Party piece
(1966)

I don't want to embarrass you
by performing just for me —
so, if you don't mind, ladies,
I'd prefer you not to see
how humble I am,
not at all the confident man
when it comes to pleasing
an unknown social clan —
so don't protest too loudly
that I should pick up my guitar,
after all, it's not quite so easy
as just driving in a car —
but if you and I were on our own
I would sing to you quite proudly
and read you poems too —

but here amongst these men with masks
I feel ill at ease when someone asks,
so please do not persist —
perhaps if I was pissed —
but right now I'm stone cold sober,
and my phobia is quite acute,
and I feel awkward as a farmer
in this ghastly baggy suit —
if I could change into my jeans,
and explain what all this means —
the blues — then it might amuse you
to hear a song or two
sung especially for you,
but here the atmosphere is wrong,
with all these politely hostile faces,
where my reticence disgraces,
so, in honesty, don't you think
it would be kinder and much better
to forget I even got here, before I regret
I ever met you in the street the other night
and we discussed the Christmas lights
and you were so kind as to invite
me to your party, or else I shall be sorry
I caused myself such worry
by sending that RSVP letter . . .
So I repeat, would it not be better,
don't you think, to let your other guests keep talking
and to offer me instead,
another STRONGER drink?

The artist
(Corfu, 1967)

I should not have let down
the little old lady
who said she was a painter from Paris;
but I was ashamed
to be seen with her again,
lest people might think her
my mother or lover,
for her breasts were drooping
from a hard winter
of whooping cough,
from sleeping on benches,
and eating old scraps
from a bin that she found.
She wouldn't visit the doctor,
she spent her old age
begging for money,
not for herself,
but for a young writer
who said he was hungry.
I never saw what she painted,
she had her work stolen,
or gave it away, so she said,
but I have no reason to doubt
that she was an artist . . .

Costa's curse
(Corfu, 1968)

The old man's wife walked out the other day,
though he claims he never beat her;
he's still got a laugh like a crazy mule,
though his mare has quit the stable.
He's grubby round the collar,
and his fishing nets are torn;
he told me confidentially
with proud demotic scorn:
"I wish the old bitch
had never been born!"

Parking place

We were looking for a parking space
in the street where you once lived.
We found a spot, a builder's yard
beneath a new apartment block.
You recognized two walls that stood
from the house that they'd demolished:
we'd parked inside your living-room.
The pattern on the paper still clinging to the walls,
was the pattern that you gazed at
almost fifty years before.
Nothing else remains
of what was once your childhood home.

Moving house,
from Somerset to Dorset
(a song, Nairobi, January 1977)

My mother's moving house today —
my childhood home for twenty years;
and I'm so far, so far away.
I cannot hide these childish tears.

I'll never see my room again,
nor my favourite chestnut tree.
The move is made, I won't complain,
I'll throw away my front door key.

My father's grave neglected now,
the old home town is home no more;
were he alive, would he allow
strangers to walk in the door?

It's farewell to the wedding bells
which sounded on a summer's day;
there are certain things one never sells,
one should not even give away.

My toboggan and my cricket bat,
old photographs and things like that.
But I hope you'll be happy, I want you to be,
and I'll try to imagine your house by the sea.

Confession of an unconfirmed man

The Dogma of Transubstantiation — Fourth Lateran Council (1215), reconfirmed by the Council of Trent (1551), Session 13, Canon 2: "If any one [...] denieth that wonderful and singular conversion [...] Transubstantiation; let him be anathema."

I have a problem with Temptation,
as well as Transubstantiation.

I marvel at the Maker,
the *Demiourgos,*
the *Poietes,* the *Plastes.*

I praise all the glories of Creation
but I have a problem
with Temptation.

Mandoukiotissa

She cheerfully put
some hairs on my chest,
then gave me
countless grey ones.

Athens, nefos and seismos, 1982

> The commonwealth of Athens is become a forest of beasts.
> (Shakespeare, Timon of Athens)

Times don't change, do they Timon?
It's not only men turned misanthropist
who talk of this "detestable town";
increasingly often now, the cynics say the same.
Banished Alcibiades concurred, and called it
"this coward and lascivious town".
Some found it full of flatterers and thieves.
It's become of late a forest of concrete beasts
beneath an evil cloud.
But since the senators are always eloquent
and anxious to protect what worthwhile buildings stand,
Alcibiades decides to spare the corrupt Athenian cradle.
The god of earthquakes, the Earth-Shaker Poseidon,
may not be quite so merciful.

Tbilisi toastmaster

We felt good in Georgia:
the *tamada* talked long,
toasted us well.

Dawn chorus, Sherborne,
for Nina-Maria
(5 a.m., 7 May 1988)

I lie awake, my windows open,
amazed at the melodies of birds,
such as I haven't heard for years,
a full dawn chorus; distant, near,
each bird in turn takes up the theme,
maintains the joyful harmony.
I've come to see my daughter:
such beauty, grace and perfect love;
bright eyes, and fresh complexion.
I feel relaxed, away from Prague,
sleeping near Saint Aldhelm's Sted.
Free minds at school, no propaganda,
no doublethink, no hidden thoughts;
even the birds are living in truth here,
in full-throated self-expression.

Fathers v. Sons
(Hazlegrove House, 7 May 1988)

In the pavilion we found the scorebooks
of matches we'd played thirty years before.
Mark was excited, "Just look at that innings —
ninety not out!"
I boasted about my bowling average:
six for twelve. Beat that!
Three for six! Five for eight!
Past glories flood the mind once more.
I turned a page, which made me freeze —
my father's hand, as clear as day,
Fathers v. Sons, with him as Captain,
his writing, all eleven names,
his team. His proud and happy day.
I got him out.
I guess he let me.

West Saxon Nap

From Alfred's Tower to Golden Cap
I'll tie our silken hammock
and there I'll lie
with you my love
my head upon your lap.

Abe and Mary

Abraham Lincoln
was very tall.
His wife
was somewhat squat.
The long and the short of it, my friend:
tall men must bend a lot.

Bosnia, November 1991

My birthday. Sarajevo.
The war is getting closer.
This year Yugoslavia:
next year, and thereafter?
I walk down the Mall,
ready for another mission.
Carlton House Terrace.
The gardener glares behind spiked railings.
He's sick of raking up dead leaves,
looks ready to pounce at a passer-by,
to engage in random conversation.
No-one has time to talk of flowers.
We're all ready to pounce, with pistols blazing,
fences, railings, count for nothing —
we recognise no borders now,
no sovereign or civil rights
where minarets and mortars meet.

Helsinki, November 2000

These Northern harbours
in the freezing fog!
Cranes and derricks
greet pallid lamp-posts
through wintry mist
which will not lift.
I too smile wanly,
like the street-lamps.
I think of ports down South, down under.
Be grateful, fool, for all life's gifts!

Plain sailing

Sailing in Stockholm harbour
I praise his skill.
My son's the captain now.

Paxiot fisherman

Where's he gone,
the man who ate lemons,
stood on his head, when not fishing?

On the ferry from Finnhamn

I want to be surprised.
It seems there are no more surprises.
Surprise me.

Covering the war in Afghanistan

My nephew is going to Afghanistan tonight. He says he won't stay for more than a month. I tell him not to get too close to the front line, to the fighting. Shells and missiles go astray. Last night the Americans bombed the wrong side, as if to make my point. It brings it all home, when they wipe out an allied village.

My nephew says he's not a "war reporter" but a "foreign correspondent". He's grown a beard so that the Taliban may mistake him for a Muslim. The editor's sent him a bullet-proof vest — it may get through the Chinese customs in time. Reuters gave him a few days' training in some of the arts of survival. My nephew's wife says he will live in a tent. They've supplied him with a generator, so that his equipment works.

There'll be far too much testosterone — all those dusty reporters desperate for a beer, bragging about who gets closest to the bombs, who'll be the first to interview Osama bin Ladin.

The winter's coming; his wife is all alone in China. I look at family photographs, the ones where we're smiling, admiring the views from on top of one of the twin towers of the World Trade Centre.

It was Halloween last night. In the late afternoon I went for a cycle ride to my favourite spot at Blockhus Point, looking out to the Baltic Sea and some of the inner archipelago islands. There's a small sculpture there, by Eric Grate. It's called *The Axeman*.

It was cold and crisp, but still sunny there, where the axeman stands on guard.

For Jack, two days old
(16 March 2003)

Hello, grandson,
don't cry, life's fun!
I hope I'm here,
when you're twenty-one.

I'm glad I'm not a Baghdad grandad
(Kungsträdgården, Saturday 29 March 2003)

Spring day in Stockholm.
A helicopter overhead.
I think of Baghdad.

Glad to be alive
out in the sunshine
among babies in prams.

Spring day in Stockholm,
with peace-loving people,
some protesting the war.

CHORUS
I'm glad I'm not a Baghdad grandad
I'm glad Jack wasn't born a Basra baby.
I'm glad I'm not a Baghdad grandad . . .

Stockholm Sunday

Lying on the rocks at Kastellholmen,
surrounded by water, gulls
and Djurgården ferries,
Gröna Lund opposite,
not yet lit up
or electrified.
Church bells are ringing,
The *Cinderella* leaves for Sandhamn.
I'm switched off
like the Gröna Lund rides,
as quiet and as closed
as the Nordic and Vasa museums
on an early Sunday morning.

The Incident Hotline, September 2003
(the assassination of Anna Lindh,
Sweden's Minister for Foreign Affairs)

September 11.
The day she died.
The doctors couldn't save her.

Flying to Sweden three days later,
the euro referendum.
The hostess said the vote was "No".

They wanted to preserve
their way of life.
From cradle to grave.

Performance art (Stockholm)

I went to a seminar
on performance art.
The uninspired speakers
soon sent me to sleep.
A critic expressed it
nicely enough:
"They were trying to provoke —
I wasn't provoked."

I was glad to escape,
to head towards home,
to sit on the bus
and look at the sea;
then to feel the cold wind,
trudge through wet-whirling snow —
that's *one* definition
of provocative performance art.

Helsinki, Friday 13 June 2003

Overbooked flight —
"seat allocations at gate".
No seats. I'm first in the queue,
but I've been bumped off.
"Volunteers for later flight?"
Got to get home,
get home tonight.
An unholy row.
Will they squeeze me in?

The radar's down
in Southern Finland.
Flight delayed.
The ground staff plan
to go on strike.
Flight delayed.
Computer problems:
air traffic
uncontrollable.
Got to get home,
get home tonight.
They will not look me in the eye —
first they let the Finns on board.
Friday the Thirteenth.
Yes, I'm stressed.

Paranoid at fifty-nine
(in memory of Roger Short and David Kelly
December 2003)

They get you
one way or the other
in the year before retirement.

Polite / aggressive
on Flight OA601, Corfu–Athens
(18 April 2004)

The tall American had to move.
The short smartarse Greek
was within his rights.
He waved his boarding card
in front of him:
"*My* seat," he insisted,
and then, to rub it in,
"That's life.
Some you win
and some you lose."
"It's no big deal,"
the American mumbled,
giving up the seat.
It was. He really wanted
that aisle-seat there,
the one which he'd requested,
the one he'd planned to occupy.
His wife had made that
abundantly clear —
no one could fail to overhear.
Legroom equals *Lebensraum*.
He gave up quickly,
quietly even.
He wasn't looking
for another fight.

Thirty words
of my first grandson
(July 2004)

Jack kisses the belly
of his pregnant mother,
says *baby*,
as he feels the kicks of a little sibling.
Jack's sixteen months,
he can walk and talk,
about thirty words:
dog and *cow*,
truck and *eyes*,
(gui)tar and *ears*,
book and *bed*,
bye and *me*,
please and *pooh*,
nothing, car,
mouth and *nose*,
shower (or *sha*),
duck and *Dad*,
juice and *milk*,
Ma and *Jack*,
and *airplane*.
He can do *woof-woof*
and a duck-like quack.
Thirty words define his world.

Kerkyra

And any stranger who there wets his lips
will never more to his own home return.
      Lorenzos Mavilis, "Kardaki"

Who can say
when it first began?
Did my father sow the seed?
From West Africa and India
he brought back a taste for exotic spices,
implanted hopes of wide horizons.
Who can say
when it first began —
when Corfu beckoned,
the Siren Island?
I've notched up
many countries since
but still we keep returning —
a ravaged island,
raped but blessed.
Who can say
when it first began?
The Kardaki spring?
That early attempt
to escape the city?
The search to find
a natural home:

Lost Paradise? —
an approximation.

New York

When you're up on the Highline
admiring the skyline
the world seems to shine bright and new,
but stroll at street level
and you'll soon find the devil
is stirring his terrible stew.

Rostock, November 2004

The last time I came to Rostock,
was November '89,
at the time of the fall of the Berlin Wall,
a few days before or after.
The professors had come to realise
they'd spent forty years in vain.
They looked as if about to weep
at the ruin of their lives,
their lost ideals, the lies.
I face my own future, arriving here,
as I contemplate my past.
My life's work too — in vain?
To all those lost ideals,
and some small achievements: *Skol!*

A nice guy — don't get me wrong

He was an all-American outdoor boy,
handshake firm, an instant grin,
proud and patriotic.
In Spain he spent his time
rooted at the bullring.
In Greece he found a slaughterhouse.
He'd watch the butcher going mad
in an orgy of entrails and blade,
chopping and slicing and disembowelling
and ripping the skin from the flesh.
He was thrilled to see the gypsies
gather organs the butcher left.
The ritual slaughter of the Easter lamb
held even more appeal:
he dipped his hand in the spurting blood
and daubed on the door the Sign of the Cross.
He'd studied anthropology —
that was his excuse.
In the afternoons he went to fish,
spearing octopi between the eyes,
a harpoon gun his favourite toy.
An all-American outdoor boy —
a nice guy — don't get me wrong.

Foxy Lady (Neo-Nazi)

She liked bald-headed men
with Teutonic tattoos
or Samurai swords
etched down their arms.

Breakfast at The Royal Oak

"Traditional English Breakfast" —
I eat alone.

For company,
three framed photos of William Barnes.

Nearby,
three men with Dorset accents.
They're here for an early beer.
I overhear complaints:
"Poundbury, Waitrose, 'Winter Palace'," they jeer.
"That monstrosity, Queen Mother Square".

Unfair . . .

The speaker takes a final sip,
burps a beery "Tootle-pip".

Three score and ten
(May 2014)

In my seventieth year.
Friends have gone . . .
Those that stay now count their days.

Good augury

When I was seven
I won the School Cup
for being "The Best All-Rounder".
Now that I'm seventy
I must admit
I have been a bit of a bounder.

The only problem / Le seul problème

Almost beaten by the effort
of forging the causeway without cause
I stop in the middle of my automatic gestures
and question the sun.

Shall I dam the flow?
Shall I let the muscles knot,
and leave the boulder lodged
in the parched wrinkles of the valley?
Or shall I pick it up
and hurl it at the sky,
then, watching its descent,
stand directly in a line beneath
and hold my breath and die?

The sea
*(free translation from the Greek
of Dinos Christianopoulos)*

The sea is like love, like Eros:
you wade right in,
you never know if you'll come out.
How many youths have squandered lives
through fateful plunges or deadly dives,
risked cramps or currents, rips or rocks,
sharks or whirlpools,
medusas or men o'war?
Woe betide us if we should give up swimming
because half a dozen people drowned!
Woe betide us if we reject the sea,
for fear that she will swallow us.
The sea's like love, like Eros:
a thousand people take pleasure in it,
but one of us will pay the price.

War Zone, Ionian Sea

Forever crossing over to Epirus,
back and forth across the restless sea,
we're like those ruined buildings in scruffy ports.
We like to reveal our scars and wounds.
One day we'll admit we're damaged goods.

In Oslo

Munch's melancholic
Nordic blues
infuse his pictures
with colourful gloom.
I am that man
with his face turned away
from the sunlit beach, in shadow.
But alienation has its own limits.
I'll never become
the man in *The Scream*.
Moderation in all things.
I'm English, after all.

Before I come to Came

Bathed in bardic light I'll stand
on Golden Cap declaiming Barnes —
my rural saint, my life's redeemer,
leader of our pilgrim band.
In his flowing gown
he shows the way
up hill, down dale,
poet of river and of vale.
I'll climb the bronze-age burial mounds,
cast Dorset words along the coast,
recite them high on Ridgeway tumuli,
spout them loud through hollow-ways.
From signal-towers they'll hear the sounds;
I'll share them with the sea and sky,
before we part, before I die,
before I come to Came.

Life is short

It's getting later than you think —
high time
to cut the siesta!

Brain damage
("Do Not Resuscitate. Not appropriate.")

They're saying that I'm a vegetable.
I know that I am paralysed
and that I've had a stroke.
They're saying I won't recover,
that my brain's beyond repair.
Although I cannot signal,
crook a finger, move an eye-lid,
how can they be certain
that I'd prefer to die?
They whisper to each other,
within my sight and hearing,
they plan to open up my head,
to let the students take a look.
They're sure that nothing stirs.
They'll soon unblock the bed.
If they'd just squeeze my hand
they'd know my mind's not dead.

Corcyra/Dodona

A Corfiot scourge!
She chatters —
like knuckle-bones striking a cauldron.

Smrt

I heard my own death rattle
a moment ago.
I tried to do battle
but I was too slow.

This time it's a cough.
Already enough.

První Máj (Mayday)

The first of May, in Líšnice.
Anyone for golf or tennis?
Czechs potter about in weekend gardens,
everything blossoms:
only the flowers are on parade.

*The Devil's Advocate
and the
Coronavirus Pandemic*

A cynical friend, somewhat concerned
about his nearest and dearest,
and vulnerable rellies,
shocked me when speaking of the pros and cons,
of the contagious virus and a *population cull*;
of the benefits to lawyers, insurers —
more work for him and his legal colleagues,
for actuaries with their algorithms,
actuarial ages, risk assessments,
changes to mortality tables,
revised predictions, lower life-spans,
reduced pension pay-outs;
herd immunity — *and* fewer beds blocked.

"Bella"

The walls close in, the plaster blisters.
The bed corrugates and concertinas.
Mirrors warp, screens crack and crinkle.
Noxious gases do their job.
Before the airport closes . . . Chaos.
And Nature calls a general strike.

Podpis
(Czech for "signature")

The Henry Moore is well located
within the grounds of Kenwood House:
an imposing sculpture, a work of ages,
but soon we mark the dribbling doodles
trickle down the sculpture's base
(at two corners sniffing noses,
at two corners lifted legs).
The dogs approach it more than people,
for our gaze is drawn, distracted,
by the random art and patterns
of four renewed and subtly varied
rivulets of canine piss.
These signatures are surely statements,
messages for Man to read
about aspiration v. perception,
and the interface of Art and Space.

*On the need to study longer
with Professor Yu Qilong*

Call that calligraphy?
Chicken-scratchings!
No flow, no balance,
no interplay of yin and yang.
You must have more lessons.
You'll need a lifetime
to achieve the Ch'i.

Hamilton haiku for a clever QC

Picture him in court:
winning his cases
wigless, in Bermuda shorts.

Xenitia

Flying back to Sydney —
no Olympic strike today
(the flight attendants' work-to-rule).
The hostess gave me
her one banana,
fruit for the crew; a special favour.
And my light at last lit up.
It's good to be able to read.
Two days ago it was all go-slow.
Eight hours of hell at Athens airport.
I got off lightly:
only two hours' confusion at Corfu
(no trauma about a connecting flight).
You never know which way it will go.
Have hope! Be optimistic!
— Maria's heartfelt plea to me.
But for now,
more bittersweet songs of exile.

Bashō, 1644

Yes, Bashō was born
three hundred years before me.
Searching for his tree!

Bashō's bones

*In this mortal frame of mine which is made of a hundred
bones and nine orifices there is . . . a wind-swept spirit . . .
(The records of a travel-worn satchel)*

Why should it matter
that we have *twice* Bashō's bones
but half his spirit?

*With Ryōkan in a
mountain hut in Epirus*

The monk Ryōkan.
Satori in Zagori.
A path to follow?

Grim prospects — autumnal Monday
(Corfu, September 2020, just before
returning to the UK during the pandemic)

The sea is quite flat;
my mood is low. Season's end.
Why bother to swim?

With hindsight I see —
I've wasted many summers
on pebbly beaches.

What a way to end our days —
in fear of more waves
or of fighting for breath . . .

Sani, Halkidiki

The hotel is built upon the sanctuary,
the workmen found a temple there,
covered it up before word got out.

Potsherds are littered round the shore,
handle fragments of three-necked lamps
that lit up the night in rituals long ago.

Our house is built upon a cemetery.
We build our lives, we build our love
on the bones and grave-goods buried here.

Potsherds and middens

Potsherds and middens:
signs of previous lives?
Fragments of words,
buried there, waiting.
I'll decipher them soon.
I'll keep excavating.

Past life therapy and talk of regression,
soul survival and re-incarnations
are not what I need.
I've lived only one life and I've left no maps:
just eroded scratchings, fading runes,
illegible lines on parchment scraps.

The semiotics of a settled Norseman.
The rough gouges of a Dark-Age mason.
I find remnants of things I might have eaten
among scattered pieces of an apprentice potter;
the shells of mussels, oysters, cockles, crabs,
alongside low-fired earthenware, cracked terracotta.

Physics and philosophy

When the sun burns itself out,
or when I'm burned out in the sun,
c'est la même chose.

What's the difference?
Five, or five billion, years.
All gone in a flash.

Brave cowards

We're all like astronauts
on missions to outer space.
That's the way life is,
each time we climb out of bed.

Christmas

This year I'm a guest at Christmas,
as if unseen, watching from the armchair,
while the family play *Monopoly*
in front of a roaring fire —
I'm rehearsing for my role
as the Ghost of Christmas Past.

The bench

I was sitting alone on a seaside bench;
a young man approached and boldly said,
"You look so old — ancient émigré or refugee?"

Nonplussed, I slowly raised myself to go.
I turned and read the small brass plaque:
IN LOVING MEMORY OF ... Yes ... *me* ...

Songs and singers

"Jim Potts, Bluesman" by CM (circa 1965)
"At the touch of a plectrum Jim could transform himself into a Mississippi Delta blues-singer."
(Michael Rosen speaking on "Home Truths", BBC Radio 4, 19 February 2005)

Musical education

I put my ear to the wall and listened.
(Dmitri Shostakovich, 1927)

The unborn baby absorbs the soundwaves,
the deepest notes of Shostakovich,
along with heartbeat, the body's sounds.
The pregnant cellist counts the time,
1,2,3,4. Four months more.
Wall of the womb, wall of the belly.
The cello rests tight against the stomach.
They practise each night, the String Quartet.
They practise each day, they pluck and bow.
How they resonate, reverberate,
the deepest notes of Shostakovich.
The baby listens, with ear to wall.

Haydn's wife
(Rohrau, Austria)

What do we know about Haydn's wife?
That she'd use his scores for curlers,
or to line her baking tray.

They told us so at his birthplace —
now it's all over the net.

Did she tear out sheets to curl her hair,
or to show she knew he didn't care?

Bohemian folk song (Volksweise)
(from the German of Rainer Maria Rilke)

A Bohemian folk song
touches me deeply,
comes to me softly,
makes my heart blue.

When a child quietly sings
in the field or allotment,
his song lingers with me,
it haunts me at night.

If you plan to go travelling
to faraway places,
it'll come to you often —
again and again.

Folk songs

Cecil Sharp he scoured old Somerset,
the Appalachians too;
Henry Hammond biked round Dorset,
all in the foggy dew.

They cycled and they hiked it,
they rattled round the lanes,
they searched in pub and workhouse
for old-fashioned folk-song strains.

They noted down in notebooks
one half of what they heard;
they cut out all the juicy bits,
and every other word.

Before Cecil there was Sabine,
a double-barrelled squire-cum-Rev . . .
he hunted down his songbirds
then rewrote the truth they gave.

There was Maud, then Lucy Broadwood,
Charles and Percy, Ralph and George;
Henry went with brother Robert,
to ensure no song was forged.

But they edited and they censored,
and tampered with each tune,
so what they handed down to us
wasn't even fit to croon.

The Reverends were most worthy,
the collectors all meant well;
but those toothless peasant singers
were all left to go to hell.

With a fol-derol-de-rol-de . . .

Žert, 1986

The mosquitoes of Strážnice
are thicker than smoke —
no wonder the singers
keep slapping their thighs,
as dancers and fiddlers
make sharp squeaks and cries.
The mosquitoes of Strážnice
swarm thicker than smoke:
Socialist Folk Song is seldom a joke.

The costumes are bright, the beer freely flows
but the blood that's been lost Old Jo only knows.
So listen and take note, look deep in their eyes:
such art bears its sting — squeals of pain and surprise.

The guitar
(from the Spanish of Federico García Lorca)

The grief of the guitar
begins. The cups of dawn
are shattered, broken.
The grief of the guitar
begins. It is pointless
to pacify it. It is impossible
to pacify it.
Its cry is constant
like the cry of water,
like the cry of the wind
over the snowdrifts.

It is impossible to placate it.
It weeps for faraway things.
Sand of the warm South,
begging for white camellias.
It weeps without target,
evening without morning,
and the first bird dead
upon the branch.
Oh, guitar!
Heart fatally wounded
by five blades.

After Roy Acuff

It's *nothing* —
the Parthenon in Athens
is falling apart!
The new one in Nashville
is better —
behold!

Song of the young hobo

He hopped on a freight train
at Faber, Virginia,
fell asleep on a huge heap of coal.
When the train halted
to offload its cargo
he was tipped down a slide,
he was buried in coal.

Blues Pilgrimage

*Imagine yourself sitting on the porch where
Sleepy John last strummed his guitar.*
(Tourist Leaflet)

I search for Muddy
in Rolling Fork —
just a plaque by the gazebo,
a T-Shirt from the Library Ladies.
The highway sign's
been stolen.
Stovall's Plantation:
we look for the spot
where Muddy played.
His cabin's on tour.
We're given a jar
of plantation dirt.
Mr Stovall's very kind.
I search for Bukka
at Parchman Farm.
The guards won't let me
near the place.
I take some photos
from across the road:
the visitors' cars
are searched for inmates.
"Rat" Hill welcomes us in Clarksdale;
The Riverside,
where Bessie died.
Rat shows us round.
Her picture lies there on her bed,
a winding-sheet.
I search for Son House and John Lee:
they've all moved on
up 49 or 61.

Sleepy John's shack
in all its glory:
in a parking lot:
that tells the story.
Tutwiler too,
where Handy heard
a haunting blues.
Sonny Boy's grave,
not far from the railroad track,
by a cotton field, a ruined church.
Thirty-five years since I shook his hand.
I've come too late to join his band.
I pay my respects
to Memphis Minnie —
beside her grave, in Walls.
This woman
could outsing a man,
play a cleaner
meaner blues guitar.
Much too late
to be her chauffeur.
Once I drove John Lee
round London town.
That was forty years ago.
At Hopson Commissary one night
I sing their blues,
Muddy's, John's,
to pay my debt,
to set the record straight.
I feel the spirit.
They changed my life,
a long way from the Delta.

The Original Dixieland Jazz Band
(Billy Jones, piano)
*(Played at Rector's Club, 31 Tottenham Court Road,
and Palais de Danse, Brook Green, Hammersmith.)*

Billy Jones,
the red-haired
pianist:
British ragtime,
Dixie jazz,
swinging London,
1920,
made some records,
played the Palais
"white top hats
with D-I-X-I-E on them".
Showman jazzman —
shakes the shimmy!
We don't forget
that he was English —
Billy Jones,
the London lad.

"A red house over yonder"
(Jimi Hendrix)

Say it's Jimi's hymn
to a Swedish house,
a wooden shack
painted Falun red.

She might have saved him,

his "goddess from Asgard".
If he'd searched,
he could have found it,
that bright, elusive rainbow.

The Killer
(January 1984)

A career in cultural diplomacy.
Met a lot of concert pianists: regular recitals.
Nothing against them: decent people, played good *piah-no*.
But I must admit
I'm a rocker at heart.
Prefer boogie-woogie blasting out,
Jerry Lee thumping the keyboard,
pumping the *pianner* with fingers, fists, elbows, feet,
humping it, jumping on top of it too,
kicking the piano stool
across the quaking stage,
standing there shaking and stabbing the keys.
I loved it then, a quarter of a century ago;
I love it now; it's the music of my age.
When nobody's around,
I still try to pick out a basic twelve-bar boogie,
pound away like the Louisiana "Welshman"
on the Steinway concert grand.
I'm good at the *glissandi*. Nothing else.
The Killer began at eight. For me at forty it's getting late.
Rewrite the syllabus for Young Beginners!
Let "Great Balls of Fire", the Lewis way,
become their Grade One Study piece:
fortissimo; with feeling.

All hail, Mrs Clinkscales!
Echoes of Ellington, Washington, DC
(for Jack, at Fifteenth and R)

> *To me, the people of London are the most civilized in the world. Their civilization is based on the recognition that all people are imperfect, and that allowances should be made and are made for their imperfections. I have never experienced quite such a sense of balance elsewhere.*
> (Duke Ellington, *Music is My Mistress*, 1973)

I can almost hear the clink and tinkle
of Duke's jazz piano
taking shape on Ninth and R,
at Louis Thomas' cabaret.
I reconstruct the place and spot,
the siren songs, the playful rags,
Sonny's drums, the banjorine.

I can hear Duke and his sidemen swing,
invited to the White House now,
performing for the President.
Not far on foot from that cabaret-site,
a long, long way from where he used to play
"*What You Gonna Do When the Bed Breaks Down*".
A suitable song for the White House.

I saw him in Bournemouth,
where I went backstage.
("how do you find the English weather?"
— "I feel no pain").
Again in Addis Ababa
playing for Haile Selassie.
The Duke and the Emperor:

two conquering lions

about to be tamed.
All hail His Imperial Majesty!
A Command Performance for Ras Tafari:
— we thank you, Duke.

I can almost hear their siren swan-song;
now and then wilder growls from the jungle.

Elvis Lenin

The cultural high-spot of my life
was not *King Lear*, or Rilke's *Love Song*,
it was when I heard, after all the bans and condemnation
my first blue-labelled record by the King of Rock
in a listening booth in Bristol.
Blue Suede Shoes by Elvis Presley.
I used to dream, one day he'd play the Colston Hall.
Raw rhythmic energy and pure rebellion!
The curled-up lip, the street-wise leer,
the Memphis trucker a new Messiah
come to save us from our bourgeois schools,
shocking Authority, provoking the guardians of taste and morals.
Tutti Frutti — another anthem; we rallied round,
disobeying parents, smuggled it home.
Life would never be the same again.

    He could have really changed the world.
    He failed to see his historic role.
    The poor boy had no brains.

Carrying the torch for Billie

There's a song by Billie Holiday —
about her love for "Jim":
I half-pretend it's meant for me,
I half-wish I'd been him.

*The late Howlin' Wolf
and the World Information Order*

This is where the soul of man never dies.
(Sam Phillips on Howlin' Wolf)

*If I ever get to the place where I can feel all ol' Arthur
felt, I'll be a music man like nobody ever was.*
(Elvis Presley on Arthur Crudup)

Being abroad, I didn't know they'd died —
Bukka White and Howlin' Wolf,
T-Bone Walker and "Big Boy" Crudup.
Jimmy Reed I read about . . .
there was an obituary in *The Times*.
Hard to believe. They must have been
very short of copy. Insufficient famous men
had died the previous day.
Of course Elvis' death was the talk of the town.
I heard about it on the radio,
whilst having a bath in Nairobi.
Frankly I didn't believe
the Voice of Kenya.
But then I tuned to the BBC —
the World Service (Voice of Objective Truth) —

and the man also said, "Elvis is dead."
I was shocked. His voice carried no note of regret.
But if the BBC said he was dead
he was well and truly dead
and wouldn't be rocking again . . .
though this wasn't entirely the truth,
because he suddenly burst into song.
Later they cried, when Lennon died;
the Media went mad.
But what I really want to know
is why they never told us
when the Wolf was going down slow.

Swedish Schnapps

I hear you, Charlie,
I dig that tune —
the one in praise of Swedish Schnapps.
You had a taste for it,
much else besides.
It just about finished you off, my friend.
Descending chords, advanced cirrhosis;
it was all downhill
from the time of your tour,
and that August session
stoned on Swedish blues.

Johnny Ace, RIP,
25 December 1954

The late Johnny Ace
played Russian roulette.
Last words: "the gun's not loaded".

The Nomad
(a song of Kenya and Ethiopia)

Fetch me my old wooden pillow,
that's the way I sleep the best.
My son return to your city,
out here you never will rest.

CHORUS:
The world is changing so fast,
new ways have banished the old,
the things that I love cannot last,
the old tales have vanished untold.

Fetch me a gourd with sour milk,
that's the way it surely tastes best,
my son return to your city,
out here you never will rest.

Fetch me my old thumb piano,
that's the music I like to hear best,
my son return to your city,
out here you never will rest.

Fetch me my old spear to lean on,
without it a man can't pass the test.
My son, return to your city.
My son, I'm not speaking in jest.

Masenko — *Ethiopian
single-horsehair-stringed bowed lute*
(Addis Ababa, July 1974)

In the mud
of the open market
squats a beggar
with a gangrenous leg.
He fingers and bows
his masenko,
playing the *tizita* tune.
What music he makes
in his squalor;
what tortuous notes he weaves
on his loom of sad laments.
But for all his afflictions and pleading
not all the refrains he invents
will raise him up out of the mud
or pay for a hospital bed.
So throw him a few cents, my friends,
half of him's already dead,
let him buy himself a bandage
or a final piece of bread;
we'll have him sing a few last songs
before the gangrene spreads.
Admiring his masenko,
we can forget what makes him sing.
Unable to pity a man so ill,
we praise instead his musical skill —
could Beethoven have done any better
with a single horsehair string
stretched over a skin violin?

Eskista
(for Burekt, Delilah, Tigist, Rahel and Rosa)

Mangoes, papaya, peppers.
Ethiopian girls:
that shoulder-dance!

A, ai ge
(Sad song at Simatai)

Below Dead Horse Pass, at Simatai,
the blind musician
sings Chinese blues.
The sliding notes
(a three-stringed lute,
a snake-skin soundbox)
recall Blind Willie's
hoarse gospel wail.
Call him "Blind-Willie
at-the-Wall".
A, ai ge!

The singer who defected
(Prague, August 1988)

The singer who defected
is listened to in secret.
His records, seized and banned,
are still played throughout the land,
sometimes loudly through a window,
for the police are far too slow —
and they love his music too —
he only did what they dream to do;
and although he's gone abroad,
his voice can still be heard.
They can't revise the catalogues
(that's not within the Plan),
so his name can still be found
though the records have all been burned
(or, more probably, recycled,
like all the dollars he has earned).
He is quite a happy man.
He, at least, is loved.

The Apocalyptic Blues
*(with didgeridoo accompaniment by Cedric Talbot
for the Sydney Poetry Olympics)*

FAST DIDJ

In his underground pulpit he's preaching
staining the flagstones with dew;
they're dancing themselves to a frenzy,
the disciples whose minds he once blew.

In his underground pulpit he's preaching
beating the drum by his side;
he prays for the brothers who lived and who died
— if only the poor bastards knew.

SLOW DRONE

In the attic, flames flare up
kindled by an antique tinder.
Oak beams, once burnished bright,
now wrinkled with pain by the centuries' strai . . . ning
to produce a single acorn,
bloom and give birth as they burn.

Let nobody weep, let nobody mourn —
we shall all in our turn
be reduced to a cinder.

Ancestral portraits
coated with the dust of generations
once two-dimensional, bloodless, static,
burst into smiles and howl with laughter,

DIDJ GETS ANGRY, LOUDER
rebelling at last against their portrayal
as sad-eyed stoics
staring at the Crucifix
frozen in poses of self-denial.

Only now do they know their painters' betrayal.

DIDJ VIOLENT
"Revenge!" cries the oldest and cruellest fanatic:
they will wait no longer for the rainbow sign,
they execute vengeance without mercy or trial.

DIDJ, STACCATO CRESCENDO
Only flames and blood are emphatic.

"Our ethnic neighbours"

"Our ethnic neighbours!"
snarl the Volvo-owning English couple
who live opposite the Cypriot Turks
in London N11.
There's a wedding party in the garden;
the discordant oriental scales
of amplified oud and tabla (loud),
climb all the way to Muswell Hill
this hot Sunday in July.
Poll-tax payers clap and dance —
windows wide open, I lie on my bed
and listen, restless,
wishing I could join in too.

The Fall of the Wall —
Begrüßungsgeld (welcome money)
(November, 1989)

I was in East Berlin
the day the Wall came down,
when the deprived poor people
of the GDR
were given West Marks
to go across
to see the shops.
They came back bemused
(for forty years had they lived a lie?),
proudly bearing
plastic bags:
I saw LPs, LPs, LPs, LPs.
They'd exchanged their cash
for Johnny Cash.

Back in Prague
Czechs rattled keys
to usher in
Free World CDs.

In praise of Bataria, the fiddler of Romiosyni
(freely adapted from the Greek of Kostis Palamas)

Here's to you, Bataria, master of the bow
    and bossman of the violin!
Greetings to you, Bataria.
    My sense of yearning's plain to see
and a deeper pain, like pining,
    is what your playing gives.
You enliven with your violin
    all the valour in the world.
There within your violin,
    the flame of Greekness lives.

Blues limerick

There was a young monk from Salonica
who played funky and soulful harmonica;
when the time came to chant,
he said, "I'm sorry, I can't" —
lonesome blues in a cell in Salonica.

Ali Pasha, Tepelenë
*(a snatch of an Albanian folksong
heard from Berat Castle)*

Where's Ali the Lion?
— Body in Yannena,
head in Istanbul.

"Na ta poume?"
(Popular Market, Thessaloniki — Christmas Eve, 1983)

Christmas Eve, a Saturday;
children with triangles,
the traditional carol.
"Na ta poume? Na ta poume?"

Under the weight of a barrel organ
from Constantinople
the refugee's nephew stoops and wobbles,
the relic strapped like a cross to his back;
he staggers along from shop to shop:
"Na ta poume? Na ta poume?"
Not for him to turn the handle,
to sing the tune his uncle grinds:
he thumps and taps the tambourine,
palms the membrane so it squeals and moans,
does oriental dances by the butchers' stalls,
in the coffee-shops and *ouzeris*;
the old refugee, long since retired,
like the listening butcher, the backgammon players,
still inhabits The City, still walks its streets,
only stops staring into the middle distance,
let's hand stop winding *laterna* handle,
when groups of young Thracian gypsies,
magpie musicians, faster on their feet,
always eager to steal a trick,
sneak round in front, beat him to the best-filled shops,
playing shrill shawms and beating drums, laughing
as they overtake him
to corner an audience with coins to throw —
but they warm no hearts, nor steal the show.
Though the cumbersome barrel organ must stand outside,
Greeks are glad to see it still alive,

still decorated in the same old way:
the *laterna* with its Constantinople label.
It may be cumbersome, but it's melodic;
the folk-songs have been harmonized:
Byzantine pins on a Roman cylinder.
The shawm-players may make much more noise,
pied-pipers with their wooden oboes piercing through the din
of the market-dealers' Christmas cries:
but they can't negotiate all the notes
of "*Kalin imeran archontes*".
They have not walked his Calvary,
the Calvary of the Great Idea.

Memories of Asia Minor —
improvisation in a minor key
(1983)

Don't put down that old bouzouki,
Tsitsanis, virtuoso!
Explore all the roads,
extend that *taksim*,
Scatter the clouds
that darken each dream.

Take me back to the East
as I move further West.
Make the rhythm more heavy
to lighten my soul:
"We're refugees all,"
your silver strings scream.

In the Good Old Days of Metaxas

The Director of Enlightenment
didn't like my song;
he's forbidden the recording –
says the words are wrong.

I refused to let them censor it
so now I sing in gaol —
I'm singing for the prison guards,
no one dares go my bail.

My songs are all prohibited,
when I'm free I can't perform.
The day will come, just mark my words,
when I'll take the world by storm.

Zagori
with thanks to Alexios Vasdekis retired cheese-
producer aged 79 from Vitsa and pre-Nasser Egypt
(9 September 1997)

Nikolaos Ninos, the folk clarinettist,
played the Zagorissian dances
like nobody else before or since,
with Manousis, Mitsos and Bekkaris
on tambourine, violin and lute.
People came from miles around,
crossed rivers, gorges, bridges, mountains
by mule, by donkey; climbed *kalderimia*.
The villages with *paniyiria*
opened their doors and opened their hearts.
In the days before the electric lamp,
the amplifier, the microphone,
before the road, the bus, the car,
in the villages of high Zagori,
from Monodendri, from Dilopho,
from Asprangeli, Tsepelovo,
they danced till late to the *taximia*,
long before they were recorded.

Corfu Blues (song)

I'm thinking back to sixty-seven,
    back to the summer of love
when Corfu seemed like heaven,
    and we all got in the groove.

I once drank the crystal water
    from that famed Kardaki Spring,
it made us want to stay forever,
    where nymphs and poets used to sing.

They did their best to ruin the island,
    spoilt the view on hill and shore,
they covered it in concrete,
    cleared olive trees and much, much more.

At first it was the Colonels,
    who helped them build the roads,
but when the Junta fell,
    there came other greedy toads.

Unfinished hospitals and villas,
    rubbish dumped on street and beach,
they raped the lovely island,
    as far as wheels could reach.

I came back in spite of that,
    to find that Corfu blue —
in spite of terrorists and tourists —
    but I got the Corfu Blues.

Just like the King in exile,
    who always dreamt of Mon Repos,
we found no rest in London,
    we knew we had to go.

Just like Odysseus the wanderer,
    who was trying to get back home,
while Penelope was calling,
    "how much longer will you roam?"

Corfu's still the place for me,
    the place to live with you.
It's better late than never
    to try to save what's green or blue.

Iannis Xenakis
(29 May 1922 – 2 February 2001)

Xenakis preferred to be photographed
with half his face in shadow.
A British shell
exploded,
took one eye
and half his face.
I can feel the wound within his music,
sense the loss, the long nights of pain,
the sentence to death and the exile,
while he relives them all again.

Greek music

The salty tang of seaports;
the *belle-laide* voice of Bellou:
rebetic.

*Bellou's Birthday Burial,
29 August 1997*
(died 27 August)

"A Communist."
"A gambler."
"A jail-bird."
"A lesbian."
Irrelevant remarks —
a vitriolic reputation.
In recent years,
abandoned,
penniless;
peddling her own cassettes
in Kolonaki Square,
like she once hustled
Rizospastis.
Wounded by a British shell
in December '44.
Wounded by indifferent friends
in the years before she died.
She accused them all, and cursed —
how she cursed her *koinonia*,
complained of colleagues
who'd deserted her,

blamed all of those who didn't care.
Embittered and in pain,
the black fish swarmed around her:
she died of cancer of the throat.
The salty voice long silenced —
the greatest voice in Greece, for me.
The burial's today —
but not beside Tsitsanis —
no space for her last wish.
"Everything's a lie," she sang —
then left; through one of life's two doors.

Gaida man
*(Corner of Tsimiski / Aristotelou,
Thessaloniki, 21 April 2000)*

The wizened old *gaida* man,
crumple-legged on the pavement,
tobacco-leaf skin scarred with patches of red,
playing his bagpipe. Made by hand, played by heart.

A frail seventy-five, a Thracian from Evros;
he spoke broken Greek; his tongue may have tripped
but his fingers were nimble,
the music ecstatic from his squeezed sack of breath.

We gave him four thousand drachmas
for sharing his art,
for giving a glimpse —
the last life-breath of "folk".

Easter 1966
(a song for Avril)

It's Easter once again and I've got Ireland on my brain
and the memory of you as I was leaving on the train
brings little, my love, but bewilderment and pain.

> For your love flowed like the Liffey water,
> so, Barman, please, mine's another pint of porter.

Fifty years ago today, all Dublin Town was torn
and Nelson's Pillar nearly crumbled
at the beauty that was born.

> But your love fled like the Liffey water
> so, Barman, please, mine's another pint of porter.

A year ago today in O'Connell Street at dawn
Nelson's Pillar nearly crumbled
when he saw our love was born.

> But your love flowed like the Liffey water,
> so, barman, please, mine's another pint of porter.

In Trafalgar Square I wait, with no one there to meet,
like me, Lord Nelson trembles, from stony heart to stony feet,
and monuments have crumbled, down in O'Connell Street.

> For your love fled like the Liffey Water
> so, Barman, please, mine's another pint of porter.

The written word

ABOVE *The author and D. K. Toteras (page 90) deciphering inscriptions at Delphi*

LEFT *Calligrapher, Beijing (page 104)*

RIGHT *The memorial stone on the grave of Georgi Ivanov Markov (page 98) in the churchyard of Saint Candida and the Holy Cross, Whitchurch Canonicorum, Dorset*

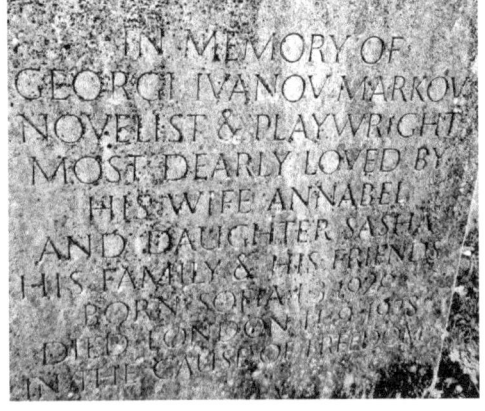

Code of practice

In Korea's oldest books
few misprints are ever found:
no errors were permitted.
Punishment was most severe
according to the Code —
thirty strokes of the cane
for a single mistake —
for everyone concerned,
from senior supervisor to
the lowest apprentice.
Thirty strokes. Imprinted pain.
For five mistakes, dismissal.

A hermit in Vitsa

Reading Chinese poems
of Wang Wei, Zhang Ji,
Japanese haiku by the monk Ryōkan,
I'm glad to be alone
in my mountain retreat.
They tell me of the simple life.
I shut my books. Where *is* my wife?

Lizzy Siddal, model and muse, artist and poet
(Highgate Cemetery, October 1990)

You fellows can't tell what a stupendously beautiful creature I have found. By Jove! she's like a queen, magnificently tall, with a lovely figure, a stately neck, and a face of most delicate and finished modelling; the flow of surface from the temples over the cheek is exactly like the carving of a Pheidian goddess. Wait a minute! I haven't done; she has grey eyes, and her hair is like dazzling copper, and shimmers with lustre as she waves it down. And where do you think I lighted on this paragon of beauty? Why, in a milliner's back work-room ...
Walter Deverell on Elizabeth Siddall, aged seventeen,
quoted by William Holman Hunt.

One face looks out from all his canvases
[...]
He feeds upon her face by day and night,
And she with true kind eyes looks back on him,
Fair as the moon and joyful as the light.
Christina Rossetti, "In an Artist's Studio"

Fair Jenny mine, the thoughtless queen
Of kisses which the blush between
Could hardly make much daintier;
Whose eyes are as blue skies, whose hair
Is countless gold incomparable:
Fresh flower, scarce touched with signs that tell
Of Love's exuberant hotbed ...
D. G. Rossetti, "Jenny"

How is it in the unknown land?
Do the dead wander hand in hand?
God, give me trust in thee.
Elizabeth Siddal, "Lord, May I Come?"

The catacombs and cracking tombs,
overgrown and split by tree-roots,
evoke the secret exhumation scene.
Lizzie's skull! Her long red hair
still wrapped around her lover's sonnets,
buried with her in the coffin —
how he had loved, how he had grieved!

When the slab was lifted, the coffin raised,
her growing hair glowed golden-red,
lit by lanterns and midnight bonfire;
men of note knelt by the graveside.
The manuscript was taken from her,
dislodged from cheekbone, layers of hair.
Seven long years, at last retrieved
for profit and for publication;
the worm-holed notebook disinfected,
dried out and copied, then destroyed.

Some read his poems, I read *her* poems.
Her life, cut short; her fame, still growing.

The humanists' raffle
December 2011

The humanists had talked about Hardy,
his poems of unbelief,
so I went to their winter social
to celebrate the solstice.

A raffle was held in the pub,
to raise money for their cause.
A passing vicar bought some tickets,
and won the best bottle, of course.

LEL
— on an entry in the Dictionary
of National Biography

*(Letitia Elizabeth Landon, born Chelsea, 1802,
buried Cape Coast Castle, 1838)*

Cultivated men summed up
the value of her short life's worth:
"as a poetess . . . diffuse".
Self-destruction the enduring verdict
(by prussic acid, but no post-mortem),
in spite of darker speculation
of murder by her cultured husband,
or by his jealous Gold Coast mistress.
Suicide? *No more to tell?*
Justice still for LEL!

Skeletons of the past
— a drunken man on Burns Night, 1959

(variations on a theme by Hugh MacDiarmid)

I wid ha' read ye gin I'd gane tae Scotland,
it was part o' my plan o' research
(questions o' national identity and art).
I read ye in Prague frae time to time,
since findin' signed volumes in a Brno library —
ye had a Scottish friend who aince taught English there.
They say ye visited this lovely country too,
an Ambassador like Sidney, but o' sicna different hue . . .
your books can be bocht in Budapest, och aye,
but no' in Prague, nae no' in bonnie Czecho.

Is it true, ye got drunk on Burns Night, Hugh,
blin' fou' on his Bicentenary?
An honoured guest like you!
A comrade in this country.

But it's a God-damn'd lie, Christopher, Chris or Hughie
MacDee —
the system and maist of what's published and written.
How do ye account for that? Wi' yet another hymn?
Did they quote ye in factories, in fields and in streets?
It's nae use preachin' tae the forcibly converted.
There are some elements o' truth, i' spite of the lies,
but the crude propaganda never dies, ne'er dies.
Jamey Macpherson had mair influence here than you,
it's true.
D'ye ken that, "comrade"?

I canna see eternal lightning, Hugh,
just bones in graves, just bones, wee bones.

Byron haiku

'Twas the bleeding doctors
did him in,
not the Bloody Revolution.

*Enver Hoxha
on Lord Byron (1975)*

I like Byron . . .
he sincerely loved my people,
sang their praises with pure feeling,
sang of their manliness
and valour.
We love our friends
and welcome them.
for our enemies . . . *these* bullets.
— E. Hoxha, *Memoirs* (Tirana, 1982)

*Racedown, Dorset,
September 1795 – June 1797*

*The country people here are wretchedly poor; ignorant and
overwhelmed with every vice that usually attends ignorance
in that class, viz — lying and picking and stealing &c &c*
(Letter from Wordsworth to William Matthews,
Racedown, 24 October 1795)

When the Wordsworths stayed at Pinney's place,
they'd complain of social isolation,
living in the rent-free house, walking up on Pilsdon Pen.
They criticised the Dorset peasants,
praised the Pinneys, their good friends —
no word of Pinney's slaves on Nevis.

Jack Kerouac

> Finally I was in Stockholm at last . . .
> I was on a seacoast town . . .
> wow, mominu,
> You don't know how far
> that sky
> go.
> *Orlando Blues*, 6th Chorus

> Dead and don't know it,
> Living and do . . .
> When rock becomes air
> I will be there.
> *Mexico City Blues*, 231st Chorus

Why do I like your nonsense poems, Jack,
your endless choruses that you called blues?
They're really not so good to read,
though I rate them as a kind of jazz,
as you wanted us to hear them,
verbal jamming, spontaneous bop,
unmistakably yours.
I once found a chorus
in a small magazine
copied word for word by a wannabe Beat —
a shameless act of plagiarism.
You wouldn't have cared, Jack:
Take a chorus, it's free! Blow one for me!
You don't know how far that sky go.

Big Sur to Bodega Bay —
*Jack Kerouac and Henry Miller
haunt the Big Sur cabins.*
*(Greek Wedding Anniversary, 30 August 1998,
for Jimmie Katsaros, waiting in Sebastopol)*

The road is blocked beyond Big Sur,
we can't get through to Monterey.
A crane's collapsed
across the bridge.
Have to head back
down Highway One,
and then rejoin the 101.
Not tonight
the Santa Lucia Climb,
that Naciamento-Ferguson road.
Got to keep moving,
got to keep moving.
So we're back in Big Sur
with Henry and Jack.
We queue for a cabin
and, boy, we're in luck,
we get the very last one.
We won't sleep in the car.
In the morning it's fresh,
I walk in the woods,
think of Jack by the creek.
The road is still blocked.
So it's back to Nepenthe,
then over the mountains,
towards Soledad, Frisco,
then finally on up to the Sebastopol woods,
to see our old friend,
the Monster and Saint,
the guitarist, the guru,

the talker, the writer.
We have a great walk along Bodega Bay.
Koumbare, Best Man,
Did we really meet in 68?
Thirty years; still on the road.
Got to keep moving.
Got to keep moving.

The Beats abroad

The Beats I met
were really beat,
not *acting* beat —
they'd faced defeat
in jail, survived,
kept low,
jumped bail,
been on the run,
far from The Hole —
hid out with saints
and Spanish gypsies;
sought sanctuary —
found peace in Greece.

The character of D. K. Toteras

"A disciple of de Sade,"
so he always said.
"Ever since a little boy
his are the only books
I've kept beside my bed,
Satan's son on earth,
the first and greatest rebel."

A joyous, savage, pagan laugh
Would burst out from his breast.

"Music is my only ethic;
even a stone becomes profound
when it hears that Orphic sound.
They thought me raving mad —
they couldn't bear to see
a man so absolutely free."

Why waste more words?
He was a disciple of Nature
who lived beneath the stars,
and even de Sade was betrayed,
when, with two gentle hands,
he started playing his guitar.

2013, the sky, maybe
(in memory of Niki Marangou)

It isn't easy to forget
poets who've drunk at Delphi's spring,
who break down barriers and heal divisions,
erase Green Lines and Buffer Zones,
who travel far, share all they've made,
though they know that life is fleeting —
artists who reach and touch the sky,
who have no need for flowers that fade.

Corfu
*Many writers have wondered whether
Corfu is Homer's island of Scheria, or
Shakespeare's setting for The Tempest.*
(Corfu, 1968)

What does it matter
if Odysseus swam here
and met Nausicaa on the shore?
Everything is in the sea,
the books can tell no more.

What does it matter
where Shakespeare set his play?
He had a tempest in his mind
which could never be confined
to a certain place or day.

One more spring
(from the Greek of Nikiforos Vrettakos)

Here in this strange country,
where rivers, stones, gorges,
clouds and mountains fight our wars as comrades,
fight beside us, get wounded with us,
here Byron died, where on these trees
Armatoli and *klephts* would hang their songs:
long gone those times, when Byron died.
For his Greece he left no descendant.
What is it they've come here to do,
the soldiers from his fatherland,
that we might tell the birds about
and they might sing to him?

We waited for them to come,
to give us once again
a few flowers
from the earth of Shelley
whom we loved . . .
Let's tell them, so they understand:
Olympus will not bend, will not be lowered!
The sun doesn't change,
the colours of the country never change,
the song is never interrupted in the middle!

Whatever Seferis says

Kalvos in Sutherland Avenue —
he preferred the smell
of fried eggs and bacon
to the drains
and dire plumbing on Corfu.

*Josef Jungmann's Paradise Lost (Ztracený Ráj,
1811) — riot police by the statue of Jungmann*

Let it stand —
the statue of this Joseph!
He knew what was meant
by paradise lost.

Let's be proud of our office
in Jungmannova Street.
Though British books have been long suppressed,
just repeat after him,
repeat after John:
What though the field is lost?
All is not lost . . .
Cot', že pole ztraceno?
po všem veta není . . .

Josef Jungmann, defiant Czech,
by translating John Milton revived his own tongue;
in spite of the Austrian censors' office,
in spite of censors still to come:
Courage; th' unconquerable will!

November cloud

*(for Peter Butter, on the occasion of
the Edwin Muir Centenary Lecture, Prague)*

On the way to the Writers' House —
Bohemia in mid-November —
Professor Butter, Muir's biographer,
sat beside me in the car.
We talked of the poem called *The Cloud*,
of what Muir meant, of what he'd seen.
The Dobříš Mansion had hardly altered
since its use had changed in '45
from residence of Reich Protector
to haven for the harassed writer,
reserved these days for the Party-favoured —
those writers blessed by the Union-Reich,
the loyal-elect, the Committee-chosen,
with three books to their names at least,
sound authors of the State's persuasion,
rewarded by a stay at Dobříš
with stipend and a stately room;
the privilege of elegance
for the price of a cribbed, diminished soul.
Today the seminar's behind closed doors;
young eager writers have been assembled,
they're being shown the prizes and rewards
to be won for staying in line and silent.
For the Mansion of Comfort is not twenty miles
from the cancerous mines of uranium towns,
where dissenting scribblers were sent for correction,
Příbrám, seat of the Dissidents' Mines.
But we were given the royal treatment,
in Dobříš' fine reception halls.

We were glad to see the guest-book there,
the first they'd had, from '45.
Aragon and Eluard, their signatures were all too clear —
near theirs we found it, Edwin Muir's!
In '46 and '47, Edwin Muir and Willa too.
Who'd come later? Kundera's cursed archangels all,
whose lyres psalmed death, praised freedom's end.
Who here remembers Edwin Muir?
Perhaps a man in a cloud of dust?
We presented two books to the lady custodian,
they were gladly accepted by the Keeper of Keys:
Muir's poems and prose of life in Prague.
I wonder what they'll make of them,
the comrades in their graceful suites,
looking for honest inspiration,
ungilded themes which suit the times,
but which won't offend the Party chiefs?
Let them read "The Good Town" and "The Cloud".
As they stroll French Garden or English Park,
casting backward looks and sideways glances,
as they search for the wire in the antique vase,
in rococo mirror, baroque writing-desk.
Let them remember, as they shred each draft:
the labyrinth begins right here.

*Kafka and Steiner, Prague,
28 March 1911*

Dr Kafka and Dr Steiner
met in Jungmannova Street
(Jungmannstrasse to them),
close to my old office.
Theosophy? *Come on*, Franz!
Give up that awful insurance job.
Get back to your books.
You don't want to leave any unfinished.

Rilke at Duino, Joyce at Trieste

I would accept an invitation
to the castle at Duino,
where Rilke wrote his elegies
and walked beside the sea,
along the track above the waves,
a stone's throw from Trieste,
where Irish Joyce
taught blooming Bloomtown English.

Die Spätbürgerliche Lyrik

"He wrote in the style
of the Late-Bourgeois Lyric."
So the East German critics would have it.
I say he belonged to the birth of the new,
the Early-Post-Marxist Renaissance.

Albert Camus visits Prague, 1936
*(collage in parallel text, from "La Mort dans l'âme",
in L'envers et l'endroit, using Camus's phrases
and their translation by Philip Thody)*

stripped bare	sans parure . . .
unadorned reality	realité sans décor . . .
What does it mean?	Qu'est-ce que ça signifie? . . .
Floundering	Je me débattais . . .
a bottomless pit	une crevasse sans fond . . .
I could not breathe between the walls	J'étouffais entre des murs . . .
Iron in the soul	La mort dans l'âme . . .
Anguish and despair	Angoisse et désespoir . . .
Give me a land that fits my soul.	Donnez-moi une terre faite à mon âme.

IN MEMORY OF
GEORGI IVANOV MARKOV
NOVELIST & PLAYWRIGHT
BORN SOFIA 1.3.1929
DIED LONDON 11.9.1978
IN THE CAUSE OF FREEDOM
(Grave inscription)
(May Day Bank Holiday, 1992)

If Markov had had
the luck of Havel,
I wouldn't be here
in this Dorset churchyard
in Whitchurch Canonicorum,
sensing that I'm not alone
searching for a stranger's gravestone,
for the writer they murdered on Waterloo Bridge,
who died for a Europe
reunited, freed,
in seventy-eight, not eighty-nine.
I say thanks to the Saint,
Saint Wite, in her shrine.

*Yang's comparison —
ancient and modern*

Like a scholar-poet of China,
posted far from friends and home,
glad to meet, sad to part,
he tried to hide his broken heart.

To some British poets leaving Prague
(at the time of the Festival of British Poetry,
Strahov Library, 25 April 1989)

Whom are we writing off today?
I'll leave you time to plot and gossip,
but you won't mind if I chance to listen . . .

"He's off the boil, no more to say."
"A good performer once, that one,
a pity that he gabbles."
"Professionally nice", the other —
"he's going to get it in the *TLS*,
it's rather sad he's got so flabby!"
"It may be an extra-literary concern,
but he's a real turd, the way he left his wife."
"How's it possible, not to make *Who's Who?*"
"I'm nauseated by all those worthless entries,
I have to face that pile of rejects;
yet another awful competition,
which, yes, I am well-paid to judge."
She's freelance, female,
banished to the smokers' seats.

The Danube — on Ister Bank

I strolled on the riverbank in Budapest
and thought of poets in Vienna.
Beside the Danube in Bratislava
I sat and gazed again downstream.
The same river flows through towns, through time,
a flood of poetry and music.
Customs men may seek to seize it,
guards on watchtowers can try to kill it.
Though violent death may intervene
it finds its way
to freedom's blood-stained sea.

A Doll's House for Germany

When Ibsen changed the ending
Of *A Doll's House*
to please a German public,
for applause,
when Nora never leaves
her husband Helmer
and cannot bear to leave her children, after all,
he may have been upset
about this outrage —
he protested — but rewrote it, that's for sure.
He has her sinking to the floor,
we hear no more the slamming door
and their "marriage" will go on just like before.

Auden and Dresden

During the last war he served with the Strategic Bombing Survey of the American Army in Germany.
Kenneth Allott, *Penguin Book of Contemporary Verse*

We must love one another or die.
W. H. Auden, "September 1, 1939"

Could Auden
have played a part
in Dresden?
Which cities did the lads survey,
and pinpoint for destruction?
Did some jealous poet
chalk Wystan's name
on the nose of the bomb
bound for Opera House?

Paul Potts (1911–1990)

*Paul Potts would be called a proletarian
writer, but he is not a proletarian.*
  George Orwell

A namesake, no relation;
nothing in common, so what's in a name?
"Paul Potts, the People's Poet" he was called,
when he sold his broadsheet ballads.
I was curious to find out more:
I, too, want poetry to stir, to set free,
to be sung by the man-in-the-street.
(though we would never have agreed
what is meant by "free").
Neither of us "hirelings" —
just singers unwilling to sell
(*sell out,* perhaps I should say).
There are lines of his that ring a bell,
this neglected namesake,
a friend of Orwell, after all.
A fellow poet. He went through hell.

The Little Nobel

Thirteen chandeliers
illuminate the grandly gilded hall.
Academicians' speeches
in polished diplomatic Swedish
introduce a Danish poet,
the winner of the Nordic Prize.
I understand a word or two,
my wife, it seems, a little more.
She turns to me
to criticize
a rhythmic composition,
audible to those nearby:
my unselfconscious and uncourtly,
most un-Eddic, inner snore.

Sharp poem

This is innovative,
cutting-edge,
interactive poetry!
Grasp the sheet of paper
firmly in one hand
and run it roughly at an angle
where your fancy takes you.
You may find you're lucky:
slice flesh, draw blood.
Try it, in despair.
Some days
it's razor-sharp.

Sirmione, Lake Garda

Catullus' villa was already closed
when we arrived at Sirmio.
Just as well.
Even if we had walked the ruins
we'd have thought less about his "Etruscan Lake",
and more of the lissom Lesbia.

Calligrapher

By the lake in Beihai Park
a woman draws Chinese characters
in water on the paving-stones,
using a brush like a pointed mop.
A whole poem, perhaps, is written there.
We watch it fade as the water dries.

Facing off the Thought Police

On this page and the next, extracts from the author's Czechoslovak State Security file.
TOP *Part of a "Proposal for surveillance" of the author issued on 13 June 1986, shortly after his arrival in Prague, labelled "Top Secret".*
BOTTOM *A document of the same date stating that the author's official function is likely to involve him in "unfriendly activity against the ČSSR" (Czechoslovak Socialist Republic).*

RIGHT *A schedule for motorised surveillance of the author during a single afternoon in Bratislava (14 April 1988), showing the code names of the agents, the makes of their cars and their start times.*

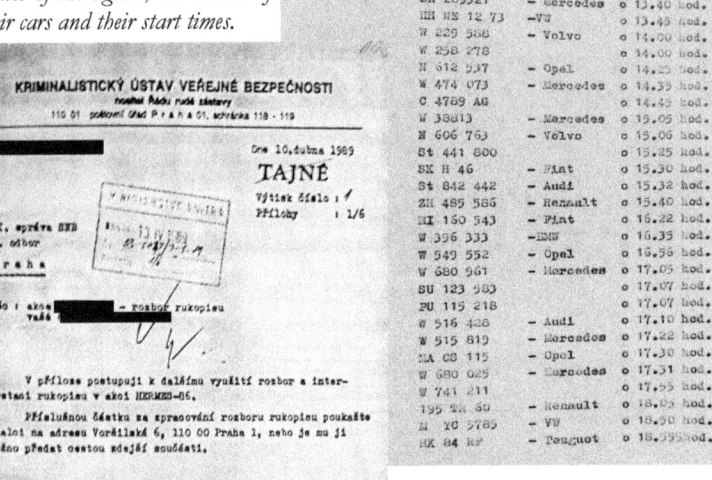

LEFT *A letter dated 13 May 1989 from the Forensic Institute for Public Security asking the graphology department to analyse a sample of the author's handwriting.*

BELOW *The handwriting sample removed from the author's office in Prague for this purpose.*

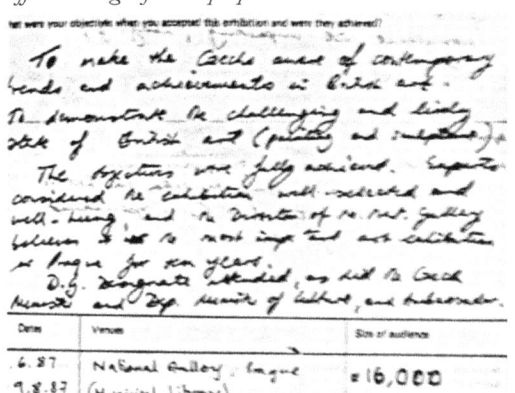

Thoughtcrimes

Like Winston Smith
I was thirty-nine
in nineteen eighty-four.
Somewhat dissident by nature,
my thoughtcrimes went unchallenged.
I didn't bother
about Big Brother,
the microphones,
the telescreens.
I was a constant subject
of surveillance —
studied like a hostile insect.
I could never come to love them:
I'm still facing off the thought police.

On a marble bust of Thomas Hardy,
1915–2015
(a concert at Dorset County Museum)

Thornycroft's marble bust of Hardy
stares straight at me, through me quite,
a yard from where I sit
listening to medieval music.

What was he thinking in the sitting?
What was he writing in his head?
The eyes tell me, "The Pity Of It"
— or did he glimpse the oxen kneel?

*Dampier's landfalls
in New Holland*

1688
They beat the drum
to scare the Bardi
who ran away
crying "Gurry, Gurry."

1699
They fired a gun
to scare the Djawi
who, unimpressed,
cried "Pooh, pooh, pooh."

A native shot,
a sailor wounded.

Three hundred years!
Still no-one knows
how to heal the wounds.

How to translate
"Gurry, Gurry ?"

To repulse the Brits
"Pooh, pooh" won't do.

"Miserable brutes!"
the Bardi shouted.

Wogganmagule
(Australia Day, 26 January 2008)

Smoked and cleansed
with burning eucalyptus leaves,
I feel connected with this land.
Fifteen years since I first arrived,
to spread goodwill, more British culture.
I've never borne arms, invaded others.
Peaceful exchange, love, respect;
we start to feel we're reconciled
at this meeting of the waters —
no First Fleet landing re-enacted
in the harbour or the cove.
Later a giant Australian flag
with Union Jack (two-thirds approve)
is helicoptered across the sky;
like wispy clouds in the higher blue,
white letters spell out *SORRY*.

SORRY
The word soon fades.
It's time for beer; beach-cricket.

Red Hands Cave

Just past
the last
suburban bungalow,
where the bush
begins.
Ochre hand-prints.
Rock incisions.
The only hints
of ancient visions.
Evidence of
genocisions.

The dream came true —
Captain Cook at Kealakekua Bay

Deified on first arrival,
honoured with the sacred cape,
Hail Great Lono, the god returned!
— the God of Song and Agriculture,
Protector of the Sweet Potato,
the Season of Abundance.
Hawaiians bowed in exaltation,
fell down flat upon their faces,
they worshipped him, Orono, Lono,
but not for long. It all went wrong.

He returned again, no more divine.
He overstayed his welcome.
Cook was tired; he lost his temper.

The violent time; no time for song.
Lumps of lava, rocks were thrown.
A chief was killed. It all went wrong.
Cook was clubbed
and spiked and stabbed.
They took his body,
they wore his clothes;
torn to pieces;
they passed round the bones.
They mocked the British;
one wore Cook's hat,
doffed and tossed it in the air.
Reprisal time.
Brits went ashore to shoot Hawaiians,
they had their day and burnt the houses.
What remained of Captain Cook?
Bits of head, hands, feet they'd buried:
gnawed bones returned by chastened natives —
sown in a sack, consigned to the sea.
The Sandwich Islands.
Saint Valentine's Day.

Diamantina Roma
and
the postings of Governor Bowen

Bowen was hated by Edward Lear, who referred to him in letters as "brute", "beast" and as "Sir Gorgeous Figginson Blowing".
(Susan Hyman, *Edward Lear in the Levant*, page 20, note)

That selfish brute Bowen
got Corfu, then Brisbane,
New Zealand and Melbourne!
Missed out on New South Wales!
Twenty years down under,
Sir Gorgeous Figginson Blowing,
too long for Diamantina,
a lady of delicate health.
Ill on the day of the Ball.
Men of the toga, from Oxford
(*Consolidate! Assimilate!*)
cared little, if at all.
Diamantina of the isles of Greece,
hosting endless boring dinners
and receptions great and small,
you always yearned for perfect peace
amongst the Corfu olive groves.
I know when it began to pall.

At Salamanca Market, Hobart

A nineties hippy selling badges
Independence for Australia —
a yellow cross adorned with stars.
No trace of red or blue.
"And haven't you been independent,
all these many years and more?"
asked a puzzled Pommy tourist.
"We're still part of the British Empire, mate,
the Queen of England's still Head of State!"
"I'm sorry you feel you're still enslaved."
The Pom turned his back on *Chip-On-The-Shoulder*,
with his Southern Cross T-Shirt, his Eureka Flag badge,
and looked at all the antique stalls,
loaded with British bric-a-brac
wondering what should be junked
and what should be saved.
Cracked Coronation mug? Cracked cricket bat?
Some souvenirs of Royal Tours,
a Georgian commode, a Pre-Raphaelite print?
He bought some really useless stuff:
three Edison cylinders, a pianola roll.
"Oh Sydney I love you",
"Australia will be there",
"For Auld Lang Syne",
some patriotic Great War tunes.
It's the sentiment that counts.

Imagined last words

(of the hypocritical hangman Elijah Upjohn to Ned Kelly, condemned bushwhacker, moments before and after Ned's execution, a taunting response to Ned's Jerilderie Letter)

Evil-minded
Thick-headed
Iron-hearted
Gab-gifted
Emu-legged
Wild-mouthed
Horse-stealing
Plough-smashing
Pommy-bashing
Copper-killing
Rope-dangling
Son of a . . .
Pig-stealing
Convict!

Port Arthur — Isle of the Dead

The first two stones we're shown
when we've been transported
to the island of the Dead —
they stand alone on the lower ground —
commemorate two convicts
who had creative flair.
From Poole in Dorset,
Edward Spicer,

who penned his moving epitaph,
soon to disappear,
by erosion of the sandstone face;
Henry Savery,
a Somerset man,
inveterate forger —
remembered by a modern stone,
a forgery itself,
as befits the maker
of Australia's first novel;
he cut his own throat,
and died of a "stroke".
They are part of a long tradition,
death in custody, dishonourable graves;
from Rottnest Island
to Tasman Peninsula
the story's much the same.
The stones of soldiers, officers, guards
(those on higher ground,
along with wives and children),
face North, not East:
face — not the rising sun — but Home.
The convicts' headstones do not mark their graves.
But somewhere hereabouts, a few paces more or less,
two sons of Somerset and Dorset share
a common plot
of broadly
British
earth.

Reflecting, unreflecting

When I first arrived in Australia
I liked the Ripolin enamels,
the slick metallic sheen,
the shiny lacquer housepaints
of Nolan's naive Kellys.
I wrote to him
before he died.
Of course, he couldn't answer.
Now that I'm about to leave
I like the mute matt ochres
of Queenie and of Rover.

I'm wondering still
which is the real Australia.

Semiotics — Marrickville

The old men from Mytilini
gather in Marrickville
on Saturday mornings
though most of them have moved away
to live in smarter suburbs.
They stand in the Square,
gesticulate, laugh loud, debate,
and argue as of old,
oblivious to the Vietnamese
who've moved in
and taken over.
The Marrickville Public Library
provides a multicultural welcome
and there's always the Corinth Grill

worth a trip for the lamb on the spit.
The grocers have stayed,
the delicatessens
still offer olives, Greek bread and feta,
pickled octopus, "Hellenic Delights",
opposite "Austurk Kebabs".
To some the population shift seems strange,
a Viet-Oz invasion, a post-modern Smyrna,
a cultural change, an exchange of people,
of alphabets and other signs;
of shrines in the backs of butchers' shops.

Diplomatic Claptrap Rap
(Cracow, June 1991)

Considering that, etc.
Noting that, etc.
Underlining that, etc.
Recognising that, etc.
Bearing in mind that,
stressing that, judging that,
having decided that . . .
nothing will come of nothing,
the Participating States,
not desiring to accept it,
adopt it, endorse it, approve it,
sign it or conclude it . . .
recommend that —
by unanimous vote,
no blocks or abstentions —
it should be withdrawn,
swept under the mat.

Suburban Backlash — Islamophobia
(Cawdor Road, Camden, Christmas 2007)

Aussie flag. Two pigs' heads
impaled on stakes:
site of planned Islamic School.

Pyrotechnics, November 5th

Economists frown on firework displays
in countries that can't afford them:
"The social benefits are few.
They can't be quantified."

To hell with the expense!
Why put a price on pleasure?

Don't miss the rockets
and Roman candles,
the whirligigs and Catherine wheels,
the showers of silver and golden rain,
the shooting stars of green and red,
the balls of fire, the twinkling diamonds
dropping down, dissolving . . .

In a flash our flight is over.
These days there's not much mirth.
So stand well clear. Don't count the cost.
Unite tonight! Light up the sky!

Venice

Mid November. It's getting late and chilly.
St Mark's Square is quite deserted
except for a solitary painter
who waits as patient as a sitter,
ever-hopeful, by her stand.

We eat in an empty restaurant,
five waiters to fuss around us.
We hurry home by vaporetto
to our hotel on the Lido,
occupied by well-armed police
and multi-national NATO delegates
attending the Grand Assembly
requiring seven thousand shields.

The cold wind
has followed us South.

The Good Life

This is as good as it gets.
Perhaps. For some
it's a grim asylum.

Sankt Göran och draken
*(sitting beneath the statue by Bernt Notke
during a performance of Beethoven's 9th Symphony
at the New Year Concert in Stockholm Cathedral)*

Put yourself, please, in the place of the dragon,
with Saint George on his stallion
rearing up above you, hooves about to trample you,
their armour all aglitter,
sword brandished high above his head,
slicing down towards you,
to split your skull
or sever neck.

Picture yourself in the place
of the benighted ,
bedraggled,
type-cast dragon
(poor PR),
when all he wanted
was to be George's pet.
He should have tried wagging his tail.

Alexander the Great

It's a pity the fella from Pella
didn't listen to Aristotle,
he could have conquered the rest of the world,
if he hadn't kept hitting the bottle.

The Stockholm Syndrome
("The party has just begun")

Sympathising with the underdog,
sleeping with the enemy,
taking sides with the opposition,
appropriating revolutions.
Identifying with your captors,
defending them, whilst held their hostage,
agreeing gladly with their grievance,
fearing those who try to free you;
praising the sand on foreign shores.

Retired torturers

Retired torturers
can seem quite jolly,
relaxing on the *plage*.
They stand there chatting,
while stroking their bellies,
their trunks a trifle large.

Paranoia — risk för istappar!

When icicles hang
from the Strandvägen rooftops,
from all the frozen gutters,
pedestrians on pavements
are warned to beware
in case sharp spears fall
like programmed missiles
dropped by terrorist trolls,
who might have been
Taliban-trained.

Paxos

When families quarrel
over children or trees
the bitterness lasts
for generations.
The feuds outlast roofs.
No one gives way
before the walls give in.

Portland tipping bridge —
the feuding fisherman
who trespassed on quarrymen's land

They took him to the tipping bridge
across Cyclopean walls.

Weighted with stones to be tipped over the cliffs,
they threw him to the rocks below —
like a waste catch thrown back in the sea.

The Igoumenos and the Saint

The Abbot of the monastery
would come down from his mountain fastness
when called to bless a house or home.
The relic of the Holy Saint
he always carried in a plastic bag.
Yes, I do mean
the head of Saint Panteleimon.

Ouranoupolis — the border
with Mount Athos

Monks in black patrol the border.
Behind the barbed-wire fence, a sign:
"No Vehicles or Women".

Acheiropoieta
(Andros, July 2015)

The Icon-Painter
prayed the painting into being,
the artist's brush untouched by hand.
Pure colours from monastic cells,
blessed in church beneath the Virgin's eyes:

White — the Essence;
Gold — the Radiance;
Red — the Holy Blood.

The divine alchemy of a miraculous art —
painted by a human — *handled with humility.*

On the need for a new Mission
(Prague, 1987)

Come back Cyril and Methodius,
the captive nations need you now!
Open greatly the doors of their reason:
they have been misled and are much confused.

Border guard

The beautiful border guard
played backgammon.
Long fair hair; black pistol.

Land of Albania!

The icons of Onufri
repay the journey to Berat.
A later work, anonymous,
shows Christ between two minarets.
Unity comes first, it states,
before the Crescent or the Cross.

I've heard the muezzin call again,
and Saint Spyridon's in use.
Pluralism is all the rage
and party politics; not work.
Skenderbeg's astride his stallion,
his long sword firmly in his hand,
Lenin's planted on his plinth,
looking rather wobbly.

Praise the icons of Onufri,
The coast-line of Illyria.
The off-shore deals have all been signed,
Chevron and AGIP have come to stay.
Albania opens to the world!
Byron and Lear admire it still
but very soon they'll turn away.

The revolution's not over
(National Gallery, Bucharest, 12 June 1990)

The revolution's not over,
not in the gallery, at least.
The paintings, stacked in storerooms,
gather dust in sticky heat.
Armed guards stand watch amidst the rubble,
indifferent to Art's untreated wounds,
to bullets through breast, through brain and heart;
to vandalised canvases, peppered with holes;
to shattered frames, to splintered icons.
I'm shown a Brueghel, and then El Greco.
Both safe, but needing expert care.
Which priceless works went up in smoke?
And the restoration studio? Lost.
I'll never invest in works of art.
Slashed and defaced; such shredded flesh.
Did trigger-happy snipers
do their target-practice here?
They couldn't have done much worse,
if they'd ushered in a gang of thugs
to poke out/pluck out each painted eye.

Neo Frourio, Kerkyra
(July 2003)

Wandering around the fortifications,
Pantocrator opposite, twin peaks
hazy in the sultry heat.
Vido island a sharp dense green;
dark cypresses define it,
recall all the political prisoners
(one hundred and twelve, transported to die),
their laments and cries from Lazaretto,
the place of execution.
I see them take that long, last look —
the picturesque view (no blindfold),

the final farewell
before facing the Wall.

Lazaretto

The good ship *Achilleas*
will take us to that isle
some summer dawn.

Along came Luccheni

Εἴ τις οὐ θέλει ἐργάζεσθαι, μηδὲ ἐσθιέτω.
St Paul, 2 Thessalonians 3.10

He stabbed her with a file:
"Only he who works
is entitled to eat"!

Return — the collapse of the Greek–Italian
Front after the intervention of Germany
(from the Greek of Efterpi Sarrou)

So we returned,
our hearts filled with bitterness,
without honours or the beating of drums,
having failed to achieve our objectives.
But when our hands
clumsily grasped the spade and pickaxe,
we couldn't find the strength
to dig the dry soil.
Someday that soil
will be revitalised,
moistened and made damp
with the innocent blood of its children
who'll die fighting to reclaim it.
Then, only then,
will come the True Return.

Pylos

The castle at Navarino
commands the battle scene
where Codrington delivered
what Byron had begun.

Ordained by Fate (and Yalta)

Since you came from a country
in our sphere of influence,
there was a good enough chance
we might meet at the crossroads.
Thank Churchill
thank Stalin
for improving the odds,
for paving the way.
Pity the others
who were fed a dog's dinner,
were given no say.

Welcome

*WELCOME we shouted
and placed our faith upon your perfidious garlands
of Liberty.*
                Dimitris Doukaris, *Secret Commission*,
                translated by Nikos Spanias

In spite of the events
of December '44,
I always feel welcome in Greece.

We didn't burn houses or villages,
make anyone dig his own grave.

Nikolaides

I think of Nikolaides
in the same school class
in Bruton.

He looked so dark,
so different,
so much older than the other boys.
He was much too big to bully,
but not too tall to tease.
Mostly we ignored him.
After the worst
of the Cyprus problems,
how easily we forgot
the seven men we hanged.
Nikolaides,
ostracised.
Wishing he wasn't
in Somerset.

Martial Law
(marching song)

The Army's ruling the country,
they're marching everywhere:
they're feeling trigger-happy,
so don't just stand and stare.

The Army's ruling the country,
ever since the Coup.
If your father's not a Colonel,
you'd better join up too.

They want to fight inflation,
and all the union crew:
they're going to save the nation
by eliminating you.

They're going to lock up lefties,
they're going to shoot all reds;
the Army's full of hefties,
who don't like men with heads.

The Army's ruling the country,
they wield an iron rod:
you're free to speak your mind
and face the firing squad.

Left! Right! Left! Right! . . . (Pistol shot)

Paidomazomo,
Prague Airport, 1988

The little pioneer brigade
of nine-year-olds from Greece,
wearing their optimistic smiles
and their bright red neckerchiefs,
heading for the tented camp,
for discussions with their comrades.

Stavrula's father

> For young Stavrula's smile, for whom
> Greece fades out in a smoke of trees,
> For her return to mulberries
> And hiving bees, her coming-home,
> I sing a song of peace.
> (from *Song of Peace* by Vítězslav Nezval,
> translated by Jack Lindsay and Stephen Jolly)

He became a Communist
in Metaxas' time.
He never changed his mind.
Then came the Nazis; more tortured friends.
Whole villages burned, murders and reprisals.
The Civil War they fought and lost.
He retreated over the border.
But Tito's path was not his own;
he went further North, to the land of Gottwald.
He was given work and welcomed there.
Unswervingly pro-Moscow,
even after '68; he never wavered once.

He dreamed of Greece,
even after years in jail,
a politico in Corfu . . .
but he missed the fruit,
water-melons most of all.
One day the Czechs imported some —
a Bulgarian lorry brought them in,
twenty-five he bought at once,
kept them on his balcony,
in spite of the dust from the smoke and coal.
Every visitor was handed one:
páre karpoúzi, síntrofe!
He sunk his teeth into the cold, sweet flesh,
the crisp red juice of memory,
the gush of juices, the life he'd lost.
He devoured it with passion,
swallowed the black seeds of exile,
gulped them down greedily.
Black seeds. Red melon.
He was refuse everywhere. Unwanted rind.
Unable to leave the mines of Ostrava,
forbidden to set foot back in Greece,
his lungs and nostrils filled with coal-dust.
When he died, far from the sea,
his only daughter changed her mind.
Stavrula smiled, and learned to sing.

Hack!
The Totalitarian Party poet
and the 1952 Show Trials
(Prague, 1987)

"A dog's death to a dog!"
wrote Ivan, a National Artist now,
when they hanged an innocent man back then
(hanged him with another ten).
"I'm a bitter friend," said scowling Ivan
(especially to those of another race).
He ties weights to the feet of those they've framed.
A national disgrace.

The Red Danube
near Devín Castle, Bratislava
(International Year of Peace, 1986)

Above the confluence of rivers
the old castle ruins stand guard,
proud symbol of the Slovak Slavs.
Long views of Danube and of Morava
below the outcrop of the Carpathians,
with their terraces of vines;
the green and wooded banks beyond,
the balmy air of Spring.
It almost seems like island Greece.
The laughing schoolchildren are neatly dressed,
well supervised, well-scrubbed, well-drilled.
They scramble around the castle fore-court;
where they'd like to play is out of bounds.

They queue to sign the comrades' book,
then gaze again at Austria,
admire the beauty of the scene:
the shimmering Danube, so wide and free,
with its currents and eddies of blood, red-brown,
whose source is the men who are shot in the back,
trying to swim to the Austrian side.
The children don't seem to think such thoughts,
nor to note within their scan
the watchtowers, barbed wire, guards and guns.
Pozor! Pozor! Pozor! Do not advance another step!
Back to the concentration camp!
Devín! Proud symbol of all the Slavs . . .
of peaceful co-existence . . .
between all peoples . . . of peaceful
co . . . ex . . . ist . . . ence . . .

The concerts in the camp are good.

Oh, rivers that divide us!
Red rivers that remind us.

First impressions of Prague
(July 1986)

Being above a butcher's shop
makes Prague seem built of ham:
smoked Gothic,
pork Baroque;
Dvořák in a bloody apron.

Right of way —
"All in Bohemia's well"
(August 21, 1988)

Tell them you are sure
all in Bohemia's well . . .
that everyone is equal here,
that education is enjoyed by all
regardless of race, of class or creed —
except the class of '68, and of course their children,
or of course their children's children,
or Christians, Chartists, Gypsies, Jazzmen . . .
Justice too, enjoyed by all!
You're free to walk through the public woods —
but not across the border.

The giants
(August 21, 1988)

Unless that wretched land be doomed to suffer
Only a change of evils, it must be
Freed from the scourge alike of friend and foe.
    Schiller, *The Piccolomini*, translated by S. T. Coleridge

But loiter not in Prague; you do not know
With whom you have to deal. [...]
                           Go tell
Your senators that they look well to Prague;
Their feast of peace was early for the times;
There are more spirits abroad than have been laid
With Wallenstein!
    Byron, *Werner, or The Inheritance: A Tragedy*

Two giants adorn the Castle Gates,
one about to kill with club,
the other poised to stab with dagger.
They terrorise the wretched Czechs.
Friend is foe and foe is friend.
Who will free Bohemia?
Tonight I heard five thousand chant:
"*Russové jdete domu! My chceme svobodu!*"
"Russians go home! We want Freedom!"
Freedom! Freedom! To the Castle!
Forward! To the Castle Gates!
They've had enough of Supergiants.

Karel Čapek and Mr Esquire,
music reporter of The Times, 1938
(translated and adapted from the memoirs
of František Kubka, Na vlastní oči, 1959)

Mr Esquire was sent to Strž
to see Karel Čapek, in great haste.
"Come to England! Why not emigrate?"
"There's nothing that I want or need.
What I wanted, no longer exists.
it's all been taken from me.
Can you give me back, what's been taken?
Can you give me back my country?
Why are you concerned about me now,
when you aren't concerned about my country?
Greet your Editor, Mr Esquire.
Thank you for coming so far.
It will be hard for you, as it will be for us.
I don't want to hear or see it.
Tell my London friends that I'm sick to death;
and now let's talk of something else . . .
Goodnight . . . *Dobrý večer* . . . Happy Christmas.
Tak teda sbohem . . . Mr Esquire."

Karel Čapek's dying words?
(for the Masaryk sisters, Anna and Herberta, after we watched a film on the Munich crisis together on 25 December 1988, the 50th anniversary of Čapek's death)

"I've been stabbed in the heart
by Chamberlain's umbrella."

Could it be apocryphal,
what Karel Čapek is supposed to have said
that Christmas Day, the day he died?
Let's hope they weren't his dying words.
Did a devilish journalist imagine it all,
or his brother,
in Bergen-Belsen?

To the Czechs

Cyril and Methodius,
Wycliffe and Payne,
gave you so much,
but all in vain.

Jan Palach
(before the 20th Anniversary of his death)

I can't agree with self-immolation,
hara-kiri, suicide.

Will a human torch flare up again
by Wenceslas astride his horse?

Václav Havel's Trial
(21 February 1989)

The Czechs don't want a new Mandela
within the heart of Europe.

Let's respect the brave one thousand, more,
who've signed their names for Havel.

The police are having sleepless nights.
The politicians? No remorse.

Black Sea — decomposition —
searching for loved ones at Kerch,
Spring 1942
(on the opening of the Exhibition, 150 Years of
Photography, Mánes Hall, Prague, 1 August 1989)

Those Soviet war photographers
witnessed the full horror:
utter devastation, unbearable grief.
Dmitri Baltermants was one
who photographed the effects of evil
and captured the stench of the squalid truth.
"War, above all, is Grief."
Loved ones lie rotting, splayed out in the mud,
melting flesh in the melting snow,
while mothers and widows
wail in their anguish. Unspeakable misery.
The recognised corpse. The putrid child.
Like a scene from the Greek Civil War.
Ancient agony in recent times.
The dark clouds complete the composition.

On the Silesian Express to Warsaw
(April 1987 and October 1989)

Cry to us, murdered village . . . Strengthen our hand
Against the arrogant dogmas that deprave
And have no proof but death at their command.
                              Cecil Day Lewis, "Lidice"

Belsen Theresienstadt Buchenwald where
faces were clenched fists of prayer
knocking at the bird-song-fretted air . . .
                   Stephen Spender, "Memento"

And here we are — just as before — safe in our skins,
Glory be to God for Munich . . .
                   Louis MacNeice, *Autumn Journal* VIII

The overnight train
from Spring back to Winter
took us from Prague to the land of the Poles.

My thoughts on the train?
Solidarity now,
a Common House for us all?

I think of events of the Second World War:
of Terezín, Lidice,
Auschwitz, much more.

Of the airmen who helped us.
Of so many lost souls.

Arbeit macht frei

Grandfather Čech stands upon Říp
surveying the landscape around him.
Something is troubling him,
a horror foreseen —
the fortress and ghetto
of dread Terezín.

Now children of Čech
look up at Říp —
a helmet filled with blood-stained earth,
an upturned urn
of ashes.

Last Christmas in Prague —
Kaprová Koleda
(1988)

I'd like to write a Christmas poem,
or, better still, a carol.

Dujdaj, dujdaj, dujdaj da!

"The carp in their tanks,
the tanks in the squares,
the squares in the cities,
the cities in chains."

Veselme se? Radujme se?
A dying fall of Ryba.

Persons of Interest

(EZO – Evidence zájmových osob StB; register of names, database of StB, Czechoslovak State Security/Secret Police)

They're all there in the archive —
Persons of Interest to the State Secret Police.
Blocked or unblocked, they're registered there,
collaborators or enemies, who can tell, who now cares?
Some innocent names, added by agents,
who filed made-up reports each day for the boss.
Nobody knows which side they were on,
those *Persons of Interest*, dead or alive.
The archive's online, you can search for a name,
for a family member, for a neighbour to blame.

The author and his wife Maria at the moment of the unveiling of a ceiling painting in his office in Prague. The painting, by Milan Ressel, featured Czechoslovakian and British icons of the arts, representing unfettered bilateral cultural relations.

POSTSCRIPT ON CZECHOSLOVAKIA

You had to — did live, from habit that became instinct — in the assumption that every sound you made was overheard, and, except in darkness, every movement scrutinized . . . From the table drawer he took out a penholder, a bottle of ink and a thick, quarto-sized blank book with a red back and a marbled cover . . . Even with nothing in it, it was a compromising possession . . . The thing that he was about to do was to open a diary . . . To mark the paper was the decisive act. In small clumsy letters he wrote:

April 4th, 1984.

(George Orwell, *1984*)

Orwell was not much on my mind when I began Czech language training towards the end of 1985. The car journey to Prague in mid-April 1986 and the experience of crossing the Czechoslovak border made me think more about Franz Kafka's *The Trial* and his translators Edwin and Willa Muir, and about Edwin's Prague poems, "The Interrogation" and "The Good Town" from his collection *The Labyrinth* (1949).

I'd also read two key essays: Václav Havel's *Open Letter to Gustav Husak* (8th of April, 1975)[1] and Milan Kundera's *Prague: A Disappearing Poem*.[2] Havel wrote, in part, of the State Secret Police, its "work-style" and despised procedures, of its "shabby swarm of thousands of petty informers, professional narks", and of the

> real mission of the state police today, which is not to protect the free development of man from any assailants, but to protect the assailants from the threat that any attempt at man's free development represents.

Kundera's essay begins,

> Prague, this dramatic and suffering centre of Western

---

[1] English translation in *Voices of Czechoslovak Socialists* (Merlin Press, 1976; Committee to Defend Czechoslovak Socialists, 1977).
[2] Translated from the French by Edmund White (*Granta* 17, Autumn 1985).

destiny, is gradually fading away into the mists of Eastern Europe, to which it has never really belonged.

and ends with these words:

Let it be known: it is not just human rights, democracy, justice, which no longer exist in Prague. It is an entire great culture that today is

> Like a burning leaf of paper on which a poem is disappearing . . .

I had been well-briefed on Czech and Slovak history and culture by our two Czech language teachers (both residents of London), who personified opposing political persuasions. One of them had escaped from Czechoslovakia in 1952. She had been part of a group which had hijacked an aeroplane and flown (with the help of a complicit pilot) to the West and to freedom. The other sometimes gave the impression of being an apologist for the "normalized system".

I was determined to keep an open mind about cultural life in Czechoslovakia (allegedly still frozen following the suppression of the Prague Spring, and the Warsaw Pact invasion), and to start by "testing the water".

Nothing prepared us for the grim and hostile atmosphere at the border crossing, the contrast between West Germany and Czechoslovakia as it was revealed on the road to Pilsen and through the gloomy suburbs of Prague at night. It was only after I'd studied my Czechoslovak Secret Service files (1,400 pages), many years after I'd left, that I fully appreciated the relevance of Orwell's *1984*.

After four months finding my feet and adjusting to the strange new environment, I bought a large red-backed imperial octavo blank journal book, embossed on the cover with the word KRONIKA. Inside, I inscribed the date, August 1986. On the first page I copied down the first poem that I'd written in Prague the month before. All the other poems I wrote in Czechoslovakia are contained in the four volumes of my "secret" Prague journals or chronicle, my *tajný deník*, a day book which reminds me now of Winston Smith's diary with the red back, described in *1984*. Many of these poems, but not all of them, are included in the final section of this book, "Facing off the Thought Police" (pages 105–144).

Kafka's novella, *Metamorphosis* (*Die Verwandlung*, 1915) is about a man who is transformed into a beetle. Our first residence, above a butcher's shop, was infested with cockroaches. I hope I didn't put an end to many unfortunately-transformed Gregor Samsas. The Secret Police had somehow learnt of our unhappiness in the apartment above the butcher's shop, and exploited it, employing various tactics to make life as intolerable and uncomfortable as possible, in an unsuccessful attempt to warn and destabilise us. If Orwell's Winston Smith was terrified by rats, we were certainly repelled by the nightly encounter with an army of cockroaches, and exhausted by the sleep-depriving screeches of the metal-wheeled meat trolleys being constantly pushed back and forth in the sausage-factory at the back of the butcher's shop beneath us. It's all in the files. Fortunately we were later able to move to a house in a much quieter and more agreeable area.

After more than three years' unremitting surveillance and attempts to infiltrate the office, the Secret Police finally concluded that I *wasn't* a hostile foreign agent, after all, but "apparently a classic model of a regular British Council worker". They reported as much on 2 August, 1989.[3] For most of my time in the country, they'd kept me (like many others) constantly shadowed and under the most vigilant observation. Apart from the microphones presumed to be in the office, they put bugs in our home while we were away and ordered devices to be put in our hotel rooms, the *ZTÚ Analyza* apparatus, the *ZTÚ Diagram* and the *ZTÚ Orion*, amongst other sophisticated *zpravodajska-technických úkonů* ("technical intelligence-operation devices").[4]

About six months after the Velvet Revolution — I heard about this in August 1990 — a nine-man team of British and Czech Security officers (now working in cooperation!) did an official sweep of our offices and discovered a sensitive six-inch microphone hidden in the wall right behind my desk. They found

---

[3] POTTS bude zřejmě "klasíckým" kmenovým pracovníkem Britské rady.
[4] For details of such equipment, see https://www.ustrcr.cz/data/pdf/rozkazy/zpravodajska-technika/rmv20-1982.pdf.

six bugs in my deputy's flat. It came as no surprise; there must have been others in the public areas too, as some members of staff suspected. There was certainly one in the cinema-cum-lecture-room. I thought of my predecessor, who had kept gesturing towards the ceiling, during our brief handover in April 1986.

I couldn't have lived in Prague in a state of constant paranoia or fear about secret eavesdroppers and informers. That is not my nature. Throughout my time in Czechoslovakia, I was simply very careful, to try to protect others. As we never had anything to hide and we were always perfectly open, it would only have made the StB listeners more suspicious if we had swept the walls to look for hidden bugs and if we had removed any of them. They would have simply been replaced. That was the argument, anyway.

There was no hidden microphone, as far as I knew at the time, no obvious surveillance device. Should I have suspected the colleagues I liked and trusted most? *We were their enemy* — that's what they were always being told.

In December 1986, a well-known actress (also a singer, translator and interpreter) was summoned and threatened by the StB. She was one of the few who dared to tell me about the interrogation. She was told she must either get to know me *very* much better and report back to them, or her children would never get places at university. She refused to cooperate, but every meeting with me — for assistance with the translation of a play into English, or as a guide to a visiting teacher-friend from London — was reported upon and included in the files.

I needn't have bothered to keep my own diary. Almost all my activities and every movement that I made on trips outside Prague, sometimes hour-by-hour if not minute-by-minute, every contact I made or conversation I had between 1986 and 1989 was liable to be painstakingly recorded. Activities in Prague were fully documented as a result of detailed reports from internal and external sources and informers, including staff or invited guests (as well as via bugged telephones and offices). My handwriting was subjected to psychological analysis.

Outside Prague it seems I was followed everywhere, sometimes by as many as fourteen StB agents and, on one occasion, by twenty-seven different cars in the course of one day (see page 106). I can now find out what meals I ate, what books and records I bought, what items I was carrying, what colour clothes I wore, what I was chatting about and the hand gestures I made on particular occasions or days. What a waste of resources!

On the basis of my official function (and their own normal practices in the "West") they had wrongly assumed and actively suspected, from the beginning and until the last three months of my posting, that I *must* inevitably be involved in developing unfriendly, anti-Czechoslovak activities; and that therefore I was someone who had to be closely watched, followed and secretly photographed wherever I went, especially outside Prague.

I felt gratified and vindicated when Professor Emeritus Zdeněk Štrbrný inscribed the following message to my wife and me, at the end of our assignment in Czechoslovakia:

> For Jim & Maria
> who were a resounding success
> in Prague and all over
> Czechoslovakia
> with repeated warmest thanks
> for what they have done
> for us all,
> Fondly,
> Zdeněk & Majka
> Prague, 31 October
> 1989

Notes

Notes

Each note begins with the page number or numbers of the poem concerned, followed by its title (sometimes abbreviated).

BIRTH, LIFE, DEATH

3. CV
V-2s were German guided missiles used in World War II (from September 1944) to attack Allied targets. Big Joe Turner, blues singer, and his partner, boogie pianist Pete Johnson, recorded, close to the time of my birth, "Little bittie gal's Blues" with the line "I ain't had no real good living since my gal's been gone". On my copy of the album that includes the song, the recording date given is indeed my date of birth. Yalta, in the Crimea, was the location of the controversial WWII conference (February 4–11, 1945) where Churchill, Stalin and Roosevelt met to discuss the post-war division of spheres of influence. From the Western perspective "half of Europe" or "Eastern Europe" was effectively lost to Soviet control. The German city of Dresden suffered terrible Allied aerial bombing attacks (including incendiary bombs) from the 13th to the 15th of February 1945. Pilsen, in Czechoslovakia, was liberated by the US 3rd Army in May 1945, but in line with the Yalta agrement, the Americans, coming from the west, held back to allow the Red Army, coming from the east, to liberate the rest of the country. Constitution Square, Athens, was the central site of the violent clashes of December 1944, when British troops fired on Greek partisans who had fought in the resistance to the Nazi occupation (see further the note to page 92 below).

4. Führer
For the typescript of the original poem as distributed by hand to a few close friends, see the Introduction (page xix). The Russian word *samizdat* ('self-published') is used tongue-in-cheek. Although this was not one of the poems that I chose to submit to the school magazine, I do not wish to suggest that there was anything clandestine about the poem or its limited distribution, or that I was a sixteen-year-old dissident trying to avoid censorship! I cannot remember which political leaders I had in mind. The poem is not about Hitler (the word Führer is intended as the plural form). Harold Macmillan was British Prime minister at the time. The poem was written after the *Lady Chatterley's Lover* court case and after

the release of the film *Saturday Night and Sunday Morning*, at about the same time as The Beatles' first gigs at the Cavern Club and the first issue of *Private Eye*, although I wasn't aware of these cultural developments at the time, at home and at school in Somerset.

7. In the kindergarten night
The children are too young to have learned of the sexual symbolism or associations of a maypole (pagan fertility rituals) or of the fruit of the Forbidden Tree of the Knowledge of Good and Evil.

9. Dagmar
Dagmar is a feminine German and Scandinavian given name, often interpreted as "day-bright".

9. Kyria Elena
The Greek equivalent of "Mrs Elena" or "Madam Elena".

10. Mother and son — Beaminster
William Barnes (1801–1886) was a polymath, Anglican priest and Dorset dialect poet.

12. Create!
"Touch me with noble anguish" alludes to Lear's "Touch me with noble anger" (*King Lear*, Act 2, Scene 4).

17. Confession of an unconfirmed man
Transubstantiation is the Catholic belief that at the moment of consecration in the mass (the repetition of Jesus' words at the Last Supper, "This is my body [...] This is my blood") the essences or "substances" of the bread and wine are transformed into those of the body and blood of Christ, while the bread and wine retain their normal "appearances". *Demiourgos* (maker or creator) *Poietes* (maker or poet) and *Plastes* (moulder or maker), are all words taken over from Ancient Greek and applied by Christians to God as Creator.

17. Mandoukiotissa
The title word means a young woman from the Corfu Town suburb of Mandouki.

18. Athens, nefos and seismos, 1982
Nefos denotes the persistent "cloud" of industrial pollution that was common in Athens. *Seismos* is the Greek for "earthquake".

NOTES

18. Tbilisi toast-master
Tbilisi is the capital of the Republic of Georgia. A *tamada* is a Georgian toast-master whose role at a formal supper or feast is to introduce each toast — of which there are usually many.

19. Dawn chorus, Sherborne, for Nina-Maria
Aldhelm, or Ealdhelm (*c.* 639 – 25 May 709), was the Abbot of Malmesbury Abbey and Bishop of Sherborne, a writer and scholar of Latin poetry. My daughter was a boarder at a girls' school, in a house known as Aldhelmsted East (Aldhelm's *sted* or place).

20. West Saxon Nap
Alfred's Tower, or King Alfred's Tower, on the summit of Kingsettle Hill, Wiltshire, is a monument owned by the National Trust. It was completed in 1772. Triangular in plan, the tower has a height of 49m. Golden Cap in Dorset is the highest point on the south coast of England at 191m (627ft).

21. Bosnia, November 1991
Sarajevo is the capital of Bosnia and Herzegovina. The title is perhaps an echo of the first line, "Bosnia. November", of Lawrence Durrell's poem "Sarajevo". The Mall is the road between Admiralty Arch and Buckingham Palace in London. I used to walk down it often in the early 1990's. The windows of my HQ overlooked it. Carlton House Terrace is another street where I'd stroll on occasion.

22. Paxiot fisherman
A Paxiot is a person from the small Ionian Island of Paxos, close to and due south of the southern tip of Corfu.

22. On the ferry to Finnhamn
Finnhamn is an island in the outer Stockholm archipelago. This world-weary thought came to me on the ferry.

23. Covering the war in Afghanistan
Blockhus Point is the destination of many walks and cycle rides on the island of Djurgården, Stockholm. It is situated at the eastern point of the island. Eric Grate (1896–1983) was a Swedish sculptor, creator of many public art-works, including *Monument över Yxman* (*Monument over an Axe Man*). It was the smaller replica of the *Axe Man* at Blockhus Point that I always used to stop to admire.

NOTES

25. Stockholm Sunday
Kastellholmen is a small island in the centre of Stockholm. Djurgården is a much-frequented recreational island in Stockholm, originally known as the King's Game Park. Gröna Lund is Stockholm's oldest amusement park. The Stromma ferry line had at that time two boats, *Cinderella I* and *Cinderella II*, which transported passengers to and from the popular island of Sandhamn and other destinations in the Stockholm Archipelago. The Nordic Museum (Nordiska Museet) is Sweden's largest museum of cultural history, a place of stories about the life and people of the Nordic region, home to over one and a half million exhibits, including both unique items and everyday objects. The collections reflect Nordic lifestyle from the 16th century to the present day. The Vasa Museum is famous for the *Vasa* ship which capsized and sank in Stockholm in 1628. After 333 years on the sea bed the warship was salvaged. The *Vasa* is the world's best preserved seventeenth century ship and its home is the most visited museum in Scandinavia.

27. Paranoid at fifty-nine
Roger Short (1944–2003) was the UK Consul-General in Istanbul, where he was killed on the 20th of November 2003 in a truck bombing. David Kelly (also 1944–2003) was a biological warfare and weapons expert, involved with controversial issues concerning the technical capability and suspected manufacture of Iraqi weapons of mass destruction. He apparently committed suicide. The circumstances of his death have been the subject of official enquiries and much speculation and paranoia.

28. Polite/aggressive on Flight OA601, Corfu–Athens
Lebensraum is a German word normally used to refer to a State's determination to expand its borders, to acquire, through invasion if necessary, more "room for living", extra territory where its population can increase. In this poem, of course, it refers only to personal space.

30. Kerkyra
Lorentzos Mavilis (1860–1912) was a Greek poet and patriot. Born in Ithaca, he spent most of his life in Corfu. He was killed in action in 1912 at the Battle of Driskos, in the First Balkan War. The Kardaki Spring is situated by the edge of the sea at the bottom of the hill of Analipsis (Ascension), on the east coast of Corfu, just south of Corfu Town. Mavilis' sonnet "Kardaki" speaks of the Corfiot belief that a stranger who drinks from the spring will never again return to his home.

31. New York
The High Line is a public park built on a historic freight rail line elevated above the streets on Manhattan's West Side. Saved from demolition by neighbourhood residents and the City of New York, the High Line opened in 2009 as a hybrid public space where visitors experience nature, art, and design.

31. Rostock, November 2004
Rostock is the third largest city on the German Baltic coast. It was the largest coastal city and most important port in East Germany. I visited it in 1989, to meet the academic staff at the English Department of the University of Rostock, and again in 2004 after leaving Sweden at the end of my overseas career. Just as the professors there were contemplating and assessing their lives' work at a time of critical change, so was I, but for different reasons.

33. Breakfast at The Royal Oak
On William Barnes, see the note to page 10. Poundbury, the brainchild of the Prince of Wales, is an urban extension of Dorchester, Dorset. Local Dorset people were not all enamoured by the Duchy of Cornwall development of the Poundbury estate in the early days. Some are still sceptical or sarcastic about the mixed architectural styles (from Dorset Vernacular to Neoclassical) and the strict stipulations and design rules, but most residents find it a great place to live. Strathmore House in Queen Mother Square has been compared, by fanciful media commentators, with Buckingham Palace and the Winter Palace in Saint Petersburg. Queen Mother Square, in addition to its grand apartment buildings, boasts a Little Waitrose supermarket and a busy car park. Drinkers and eaters who frequent The Royal Oak in Dorchester are probably not regulars at The Duchess of Cornwall Inn in Poundbury. Outside the Duchess of Cornwall and the Square is Philip Jackson's statue of the Queen Mother, which was unveiled by Queen Elizabeth II in October 2016. The Royal Party included the Duke of Edinburgh, the Prince of Wales and the Duchess of Cornwall, who also visited the Waitrose store and pulled a pint at the inn named in her honour.

34. The only problem / Le seul problème
Le mythe de Sisyphe: essai sur l'absurde by Albert Camus begins, "Il n'y a qu'un problème philosophique vraiment sérieux: c'est le suicide" — "There is but one truly philosophical problem and that is suicide" (*The Myth of Sisyphus*, translated by Justin O'Brien, 1955).

NOTES

35. The sea
Dinos Christianopoulos (1932–2020) was a noted Greek poet of Thessaloniki, with a scholarly enthusiasm for rebetiko music (see the note below to pages 70–71).

35. War Zone, Ionian Sea
Epirus, in northwestern Greece, borders Albania to the north. Its capital city is Ioannina, and Igoumenitsa is its chief port. For more than fifty years we have made frequent ferry crossings to and fro between Corfu and Igoumenitsa. I have written extensively on the region in my book, *The Ionian Islands and Epirus, a Cultural History* (Signal Books, Oxford; Oxford University Press, New York; 2010).

36. In Oslo
Edvard Munch (1863–1944), Norwegian painter. The Munch Museum in Oslo is exceptionally important and comprehensive.

36. Before I come to Came
On Golden Cap, see the note to page 20. On William Barnes, see the note to page 10. William Barnes is buried in St Peter's Churchyard, Winterborne Came, Dorset. The name Came comes "from the possession of this manor by the Abbey of Saint Stephen at Caen (in Normandy), from the time of William the Conqueror" (*Dorset place names: their origin and meanings* by A. D. Mills, Southhampton, 1986). The Ridgeway, or here the South Dorset Ridgeway between Dorchester and Weymouth is "not just an ancient trackway but a ridge of high land that has attracted people for thousands of years — a special place to celebrate life and bury their dead" (website of the Dorset Area of Outstanding Natural Beauty).

38. Corcyra/Dodona
Corcyra is the Latin form of Korkyra, an Ancient Greek city and colony of Corinth, now Kerkyra (Corfu). Dodona (present-day Dodoni) was the oldest Greek oracle, an ancient sanctuary in Epirus, mentioned by Homer and Herodotus. The brazen scourge of three thongs, the cauldron and the knuckle bones (*astragaloi*) are mentioned in many sources describing the instruments used for making prophecies by means of the sounds produced by the wind moving the suspended bones, or the thongs of the Corcyraean scourge striking a circle of bronze vessels.

38. Smrt
Smrt is the Czech word for death.

38. První Máj (Mayday)
Líšnice is a town in Bohemia with a famous golf club (founded 1928) and it was the location of the Diplomatic Club in the Communist years.

39. "Bella"
A poem written at the Bella Venezia Hotel in Corfu, after a disturbing vision.

40. Podpis
Henry Moore (1898–1986), world-renowned British sculptor whose *Two Piece Reclining Figure*, can be seen outdoors in the grounds of Kenwood House on the edge of Hampstead Heath, London. When the poem was written, the sculpture was not protected, as it is now, by railings.

40. On the need to study longer with Professor Yu Qilong
Yu Qilong was a Chinese professor at the Beijing Language and Culture Centre for Diplomatic Missions. I took some elementary calligraphy lessons with him in Beijing. He was widely acknowledged for his attainments in Beijing Opera, Chinese Painting, and Calligraphy. In Ancient Chinese philosophy, *yin* and *yang* are apparently contrary forces or principles which may in fact be complementary, like dark and light, male and female. Ch'i (or Qi) refers to the circulating life energy that is considered to be inherent in all things.

41. Hamilton haiku for a clever QC
QC is the abbreviation for a Queen's Counsel, otherwise known as "a silk" — a barrister who has been appointed, on the basis of merit, and who is entitled to wear a special silk gown and wig as a senior counsel in court cases.

41. Xenitia
Xenitia (literally "being in a foreign land") is a difficult concept to translate with precision. It evokes the pain and sorrow of someone forced into lengthy periods of economic migration (often alone, without other members of the family), or of a person working overseas, among foreigners, suffering profound homesickness, in a state of exile as much enforced by circumstances as willingly self-imposed.

42. Bashō, 1644
Bashō (1644–1694) was one of the most influential Japanese poets. His disciples planted a banana tree (*bashō*) for him as a gift to provide him with shade beside his hut, and he adopted the name of the tree as his pseudonym.

42. Bashō's bones
Bashō wrote that the human body has one hundred bones and nine openings. In fact the body has a just over two hundred bones.

42. With Ryōkan in a mountain hut in Epirus
Ryōkan (1758–1831) was a much-loved Japanese poet, a Soto Zen Buddhist hermit monk. On Epirus see the note to page 35 ("War Zone"). Satori is a Japanese Buddhist term for *awakening* (not to be confused with the term "woke"!). Zagori is the name of a region of forty-six stony villages or traditional settlements (*Zagorochoria*) in the Pindus mountains of Epirus, in northwestern Greece. It is an area of great natural beauty, unspoilt nature and traditional architecture.

43. Sani, Halkidiki
Sani is a settlement (now a highly developed tourist resort) on Kassandra, the westernmost leg of the Halkidiki peninsula in northern Greece

44. Physics and philosophy
C'est la même chose: it's the same thing

45. Christmas
"The Ghost of Christmas Past" is one of the spirits who visit Ebenezer Scrooge in Charles Dickens' novella *A Christmas Carol* (1843).

SONGS AND SINGERS

50–51. Folk songs
Although this satirical song sounds unfairly critical of the collectors, I must profess the greatest admiration for their important work, their individual sacrifices and vital contributions. Cecil Sharp (1859–1924) was a collector and transcriber of the folk songs of the British Isles (especially Somerset) and of Appalachia. He was a leading light in the folk song revival. Some of the songs he collected were bowdlerised for use in school song books. Henry Hammond (1866–1910) and his brother Robert Hammond (1868–?) were folk song collectors, concentrating mainly on Dorset. They would tour the county by bicycle. "All in the foggy dew" is an allusion to the famous folk song, "The foggy dew", which is known throughout the British Isles and in the USA, and has been collected and recorded in many different versions, some of them bowdlerised on account of the ballad's double meanings. "Sabine" denotes the Reverend Sabine Baring-Gould (1834–1924) who was a

prolific author, an Anglican priest, a hymn-writer ("Onward, Christian Soldiers", for example), and an influential folk song collector (mainly in Devon and Cornwall). He felt obliged to alter the words of some of the songs, but kept notes of the original lyrics. "Maud" is Maud Karpeles (1885–1976), an author and folk song collector who devoted herself to the English Folk Song and Dance Society. As his secretary, she travelled and collaborated with Cecil Sharp and later collected many songs in Newfoundland on her own. Lucy Broadwood (1858–1929) was an author and collector of songs from around the country, including the Scottish Highlands and Sussex. She contributed to the Early Music Movement as well as the Folk Song Society, of which she was elected President towards the end of her life. "Percy" is Percy Grainger (1882–1961), a composer, performer and folk song collector. Born in Australia, he moved to England in 1901, where he developed his interest in folk song, collecting songs in Lincolnshire. He had great respect for the skills of the singers, and for their individual styles. He moved to the USA in 1914 and became an American citizen. "Charles" is Charles Marson (1859–1914), an author, Christian Socialist, Anglican priest (Vicar of Hambridge) and folk song collector. He collaborated (as lyrics editor) with Cecil Sharp on the three volumes of *Folk Songs from Somerset*. They fell out in 1906. "Ralph" is Ralph Vaughan Williams (1872–1955), a major British composer, creator of the nationalist stream in English music, who introduced strains of folk song into his compositions. He collected many folk songs in Essex, Suffolk, Norfolk and Yorkshire. He became President of the English Folk Dance and Song Society. One of my favourite works is his setting of William Barnes' poem, "Linden Lea". "George" is George Butterworth (1885–1916) and/or George Gardiner (*c*.1852–1910): Butterworth was a composer (*A Shropshire Lad*) and folk song collector, mainly in Sussex, who was killed in WWI at the first Battle of the Somme; Gardiner was a folk song collector with a special interest in Hampshire, although he was also more of an internationalist than his contemporaries. "Henry went with brother Robert" refers to the Hammonds (see above).

52. Žert, 1986

Žert is Czech for a joke or "the joke". This is also a reference to the novel, *The Joke* (*Žert*), by Milan Kundera. There is a passage in the novel where Kundera satirizes the Czechoslovak Communist Party's appropriation and exploitation of folksong and folk dance. I was reminded of it at the Stražnice (South Moravia) International Folklore Festival. It is claimed

NOTES

to be "the oldest and largest folklore festival in Europe". The first festival took place in 1946. "Old Jo" refers to Stalin.

53. After Roy Acuff

Roy Acuff (1903–1952) was an influential and much loved American country singer and fiddler, hugely popular during WWII, and an important influence on Hank Williams. The Parthenon in Nashville (built 1897) is a full-scale replica of the ancient Parthenon in Athens.

54–55. Blues Pilgrimage

"Muddy" is Muddy Waters (real name McKinley Morganfield $c.$1913–1983), who often stated that he was born in Rolling Fork, Mississippi. He grew up on Stovall Plantation, where he lived for around thirty years, from the age of three, and where he was first recorded in 1941–42. "Bukka" is Bukka White (1906–1977), most famous for his powerful song "Fixin' to die Blues". He served time at Mississippi State Penitentiary (in Parchman Farm, the State Penal Farm). "Rat" Hill was the owner of The Riverside Hotel, where Bessie Smith died after a car accident, at a time when it was a hospital for black people. Son House (1902–1988), one of the most intense of Blues singers, was born near Clarksdale; he too spent time in Parchman Farm, in 1928–29. "John Lee" is John Lee Hooker ($c.$1917–2001), one of the greatest Blues singers. I first got to know him in 1964, when he recorded a Blues soundtrack commentary for an Oxford student film I had written and directed. Highways 49 and 61 were legendary Blues highways. "Sleepy John" is Sleepy John Estes ($c.$1899–1977) from Ripley and Brownsville, Tennessee, and was known for his moving autobiographical Blues. I had the opportunity to talk to him briefly in 1964, mostly about his song "Rats in my kitchen". Tutwiler, Mississippi is another legendary place in the early history of the Blues, a railway crossing township where "Handy" (W. C. Handy, 1873–1958) first heard the sound of a slide guitarist in 1903. Handy is credited as the "Father of the Blues", a jazz composer, arranger and instrumentalist, famous for "St. Louis Blues", "The Memphis Blues" and "Beale Street Blues". "Sonny Boy" is Sonny Boy Williamson II, the adopted professional name of Rice Miller (1912–1965), a Blues singer and harmonica player who influenced many British musicians. Memphis Minnie, born Lizzie Douglas (1897–1973), was an outstanding Blues guitarist and a feisty singer ("Me and my chauffeur" is one of her best-remembered songs). The New Hope Baptist Church Cemetery, in Walls, Mississippi is the location of her burial site, where I went to pay my respects. The Hopson Plantation Commissary is in

NOTES

Clarksdale, Mississippi. I was thrilled to perform there one night, impromptu, with a borrowed guitar, as a tribute to some of my favourite Blues artists who had greatly enriched my life. I have the recording to prove it! "The Delta" refers to the Mississippi Delta region, one of the most important areas in the story of the Blues. After the "Great Migration" from the Southern States to the Northern cities, Delta Blues had a huge influence on both Country and Chicago and Detroit Urban Blues, as well as Rock 'n' roll.

56. The Original Dixieland Jazz Band
Billy Jones (born 1892) was a pioneering English pianist familiar with ragtime music who was invited to play with the Original Dixieland Jazz Band in May 1919, when they were performing in England. The ODJB was the first band to make — in 1917 — a commercial jazz recording. Billy played with the band on nine recorded numbers in January 1920.

56. "A red house over yonder"
Falun red is the traditional deep red colour of Swedish wooden cottages. The "goddess from Asgard" was a Swedish girlfriend, whom Jimi Hendrix had first met, in Sweden, in 1968.

57. The Killer
"The Killer" is the nickname of Jerry Lee Lewis (born 1935), the Rock 'n' roll and Country singer and pianist, whose first recordings for the Sun label in Memphis took place in 1956. I have visited his ranch in Nesbit, Mississippi. "Killer" was apparently a common slang term during his youth in Ferriday, Louisiana. I also visited his childhood home there and later sent his sister a copy of this poem.

58–59. All hail, Mrs Clinkscales!
When he was only seven years old, Ellington took his first piano lessons with a teacher called Marietta Clinkscales. "Jack" is the name of my first grandson, whose family lived on R Street NW near the intersection with Fifteenth Street, just a few blocks from "Ninth and R" where Louis Thomas' cabaret was once located, in a building at 901 R Street NW in the Shaw Historic District. This building was demolished in August 2002, in spite of the protests of preservationists, who had planned to make it part of the African American Heritage Trail. Bournemouth in Dorset is where the interview with Duke Ellington, in which I participated with three other undergraduates from Wadham College Oxford, took place — in Duke's dressing room. It was published in the independent Oxford student magazine, *Oxymoron* 2 (December 1965.)

Ras Tafari, or Ras Tafari Makonnen (1892–1975) was the Emperor of Ethiopia from 1930 to 1974, reigning as His Imperial Majesty Haile Selassie the First. I was present when the Duke played for the Emperor at a Command Performance in Addis Ababa in 1973. The Emperor was deposed on 12 September, 1974. The Marxist Provisional Military Government executed sixty former ministers and officials by firing squad on 23 November 1974. I was in Addis, playing a game of cricket at the General Wingate School, and we could all clearly hear the sounds of the continuous gunshots. The former Emperor died in August 1975. It was widely suspected that he had been strangled in his bed — hence the "wilder growls from the jungle" and the association in my mind with Duke Ellington's famous "jungle sound" of the late 1920's.

59. Elvis Lenin
Colston Hall was Bristol's main concert hall, where I attended many jazz and Rock 'n' roll concerts as a teenager. In September 2020 the hall changed its name to Bristol Beacon. Edward Colston was a wealthy seventeenth-century English merchant, MP and philanthropist who was also involved in the slave trade. His bronze memorial statue was pulled down and cast into Bristol Harbour on 7 June, 2020, during a Black Lives Matter protest.

60. The late Howlin' Wolf and the World Information Order
Howlin' Wolf, real name Chester Burnett (1910–1976), was probably my favourite Blues singer; there are few songs as compelling as "Smokestack lightnin'". I was fortunate to meet him in 1964. Extracts from my backstage interview with the Wolf were included in my article, "Backstage at the Blues Festival" (*Isis* 1478, 28 November, 1964). "World Information Order", or The New World Information and Communication Order, was a topic widely discussed in media and development agencies in the 1970s and 1980s in the context of alleged media imperialism, the inequality of media and broadcast equipment access, and culturally insensitive professional training and news coverage related to the so-called Third World and the North–South divide. It was a preoccupation during my television and film production years in Ethiopia and Kenya (1971–1978) and as a media consultant and editor of the journal *Educational Broadcasting International* (1978–1980). My article, "Is there an International Film Language?" (*Sight and Sound* 48.2, Spring 1979), also dealt with aspects of the subject. Sam Phillips (1923–2003) was the visionary record producer who founded the Sun Studio and record label in Memphis, Tennessee. He recorded and discovered artists

like Howlin' Wolf, Elvis Presley, Jerry Lee Lewis, Carl Perkins and Johnny Cash. On Bukka White see note to pages 54–55 above. T. Bone Walker (1923–2003) was a highly influential electric Blues guitar innovator and important Blues singer, famous for such songs as "Call it Stormy Monday" and "Cold, Cold Feeling". Arthur "Big Boy" Crudup (1905–1974) was another Delta bluesman who recorded the original versions of "That's all right", "So glad you're mine", "My baby left me" — all covered by Elvis Presley — as well as Blues classics such as "Death Valley Blues", "Rock me Mamma" and "Mean ol' Frisco". Jimmy Reed (1925–1976) was a Rhythm 'n' Blues singer and harmonica player whose songs and backings had an infectious slow boogie beat. He had hits with songs later covered by The Rolling Stones, Elvis Presley and many others — including "Big Boss man", "Honest I do", "Bright Lights, Big City" and "Baby what do you want me to do?" His dependence on alcohol did not improve his musical skills, speech or moods, as I was to witness when he provoked a stormy backstage row with Big Joe Williams and John Lee Hooker during a recorded group interview in Bristol, England, in 1969.

61. Swedish Schnapps
"Swedish Schnapps" is a Charley Shavers composition, recorded by the Charlie Parker Quintet in 1951. Charlie had arrived in Sweden in November 1950 and toured for three weeks. He died in 1955.

61. Johnny Ace, RIP, 25 December 1954
Johnny Ace (1929–1954) was an American Rhythm 'n' Blues artist, who shot and killed himself by mistake. It was widely reported that he had been playing Russian roulette, but a witness later claimed that he'd been drinking and fooling around with his gun, thinking it wasn't loaded. His biggest hit record (posthumous) was "Pledging my love".

62. The Nomad
The Maasai diet is highly dependent on cows' milk, or cows' milk mixed with blood. They use gourds to carry sour milk when on the move. African thumb-pianos vary in size and name. They are small portable plucked instruments (idiophones) with a wooden resonator or sound box on which the metal keys (prongs or tines) of different lengths are fixed and played with both thumbs.

63. Masenko — Ethiopian single-horsehair-stringed bowed lute
Tizita (or tezeta) is the name for a nostalgic song and/or musical mode in Ethiopian folk music or jazz, involving traditional instruments. I once

took lessons from a masenko master, Alemaya Fanta.

64. Eskista
Eskista is a sensuous Ethiopian dance.

64. A, ai ge (Sad song at Simatai)
Dead Horse Pass is a strategic pass in the eastern part of the Great Wall of China. Blind Willie Johnson (1897–1945) was a Texan evangelical Gospel singer and street guitarist.

65. The singer who defected
I had in mind the popular singer Waldemar Matuška, who left Czechoslovakia in 1986 with his wife and settled in the USA. In Czechoslovakia his songs were banned. "He, at least, is loved" is a deliberate echo and variation of the line "We at least love" from Ewald Osers' translation of a poem from *The Plague Column* by Jaroslav Seifert (London, 1979).

66–67. The Apocalyptic Blues
The Sydney Poetry Olympics were developed by the Greek–Australian performance poet Komninos Zervos. Cedric Talbot is an Australian didgeridoo player. I once performed several poems, including this one, at the Lyric Theatre, Sydney, arranged for his expressive didj accompaniment. The occasion was the Sydney Poetry Olympics. For three consecutive years, 1995–1997, I was invited to be one of the judges. In 1997 they asked the judges to perform too (the other judges then were Chin Woon Ping and Jill Jones). Cedric belongs to the Bundjalung people, Aboriginal Australians whose language was once more widely spoken in the northern coastal area of New South Wales and southeast Queensland. He has been a performer since the age of eleven, first with Awabakal Dance Troupe and then with Bahtabah Aboriginal Dance Troupe. He used to tour schools throughout Australia, raising awareness and introducing children to the richness of Aboriginal culture, using didgeridoo, language, body painting, dance, song and artefacts, as well as Dreamtime and personal stories. The "rainbow sign" alludes to the spiritual: "God gave Noah the rainbow sign / No more water, the fire next time", and thus also, at one remove, to James Baldwin's essay *The Fire Next Time* and the US Civil Rights movement. I wrote an earlier version of this poem as a university student in the early 1960s.

NOTES

69. In praise of Bataria, the fiddler of Romiosyni
Romiosyni can signify the inextinguishable Greek spirit or soul, the sense of allegiance, belonging, identity and ideals of Hellenism, the unifying bonds of a common language and culture shared by the *Romioi*, the Greek-speaking Christians of the Eastern Roman Empire (known retrospectively as Byzantium) — or it can suggest the essence of Greekness, the flame of the struggle for freedom, as evoked by Ritsos' poem *Romiosyni*. "Palamas" is Kostis Palamas (1859–1943), a prolific poet and man of letters, considered a major national poet, a poet of Hellenism. His works include the book-length poems *The Twelve Words of the Gypsy* and *The King's flute*, both translated into English by Theodore Stephanides and George Katsimbalis.

69. Ali Pasha, Tepelenë
Ali Pasha (1740–1822). The life of Ali Pasha, "The Lion of Yannena", is too full of incident, myth and political intrigue to summarise here. An Albanian Muslim in the Ottoman Empire, he governed large areas of Epirus, Thessaly and Macedonia, waged war on the Souliots, defied the Sultan and ruled as the tyrannical chief of a virtually independent state. Politically astute, able to play one European power off against another, he indirectly created opportunities for the Greeks to further their revolutionary ambitions. A brigand chief in his youth, he was a moderniser in some respects. Yannena (more properly Ioannina) was the location of his court and an important centre of education. He was capable of great charm *and* extreme, despotic cruelty and guilty of massacre. The Sultan in Istanbul eventually decided that enough was enough. Ali had overreached himself, so he was cornered and killed in Ioannina. After he was shot, his head was cut off and subsequently presented to Sultan Mahmud II in Istanbul. His body was buried in a tomb close to the Fethiye Mosque in the precinct of the ruins of Ioannina Castle. Ali Pasha was born in, or near, Tepelenë (or Tepelena) in Albania, where Lord Byron visited him. There is a fine statue of Ali in the town. Berat Castle is impressively and strategically located, a fortress on a hill. I was taken there courtesy of the Albanian Ministry of Culture on my first official visit to Albania in 1991, before Britain had re-established diplomatic relations with Tirana. My visit was a first step towards the establishment of friendly cultural and educational links between the two countries.

70–71. "Na ta poume?"
The title, meaning "Shall we sing them?", is asking permission to sing

NOTES

Christmas carols in the expectation of monetary reward. "The City" denotes Constantinople, which fell to the Ottoman Turks in 1453. The Greeks have always dreamed of retaking it one day. Since the Asia Minor disaster of 1922, and later pogroms and expulsions, the Greek presence in the city has been greatly diminished. *Laterna* is the Greek (and Turkish) for a barrel organ. *Kalin imeran archontes* is a traditional Greek Christmas carol, "Good day, Archons". Archons were powerful men holding important public positions, wealthy enough to reward or tip the carol singers — was there perhaps an element of false respect or flattery involved?

71. Memories of Asia Minor
A *taksim* is an improvised introduction to a song or instrumental piece. Vassilis Tsitsanis was a much-loved bouzouki player and composer. He died in January 1984 in a London hospital.

72. In the Good Old Days of Metaxas
General Ioannis Metaxas (1871–1941) served as Prime Minister of Greece from 1936 to 1941, but suspended parliament and ruled as a dictator. He is, though, respected for his bold defiance of Mussolini who, in 1940, had demanded that Italian forces be allowed to occupy parts of Greece. His alleged one-word telegram in reply is celebrated every year on Ochi ("No") Day, the 28th of October.

73. Zagori
On Zagori see the note to page 42 ("With Ryōkan...") above. Nikolaos Ninos, Kostas Manousis, Demetrios (or Mitsos) Rountas (also known as Mitsos Ganas), and Athanasios Bekkaris were noted early twentieth-century musicians in Zagori.

74. Corfu Blues (song)
On the Kardaki Spring see the note to page 30 above. Mon Repos is a nineteenth century neoclassical mansion, built in 1828–1831 during the period of the British Protectorate by Sir Frederick Adam, Lord High Commissioner. When Great Britain ceded the Ionian Islands to Greece in 1864, the villa became the summer residence of the Greek Royal Family, and remained such until 1967. Prince Philip, Duke of Edinburgh was born at Mon Repos in 1921. After King Constantine II escaped from Greece in 1967 to live in exile in London, Mon Repos was confiscated by the Greek State, in spite of the former King's protestations and prolonged legal challenges that it was the royal family's inherited private property.

76–77. Greek music / Bellou's Birthday Burial

Sotiria Bellou (1921–1997) was an outstanding female rebetiko singer. "Rebetic" is a quality of a *rebetis* or *rebetissa* (male or female musicians or associates of the genre), and of the outsider lifestyle, behaviour and anti-establishment attitudes associated with them. The songs often dealt with the experiences of those who lived on the fringes of "polite" society (prison, poverty, hashish, physical violence, political activism, prostitution, etc.). Many of them had come to Greece from Smyrna and other parts of Asia Minor as refugees in 1922–1923. "Rebetic" also implies an admirably free, nonconformist, rebellious way of life. *Rizospastis* is the Greek Communist Party newspaper. *Koinonia* means society, community, social group or network. On "December 44", see the note to page 92 below. The phrase "life's two doors" is a reference to the song made famous by Stelios Kazantzides and also sung by Sotiria Bellou, "Life has two doors", also known as "My last evening", lyrics by Eftichia Papayianopoulou.

77. Gaida man

The *gaida* is a Greek and more widely southeast European or Balkan bagpipe. An ancient folk instrument, the Macedonian and Thracian *gaida* typically has a medium pitch. Sheepskin or goatskin is used for the bag; there is a single-reed chanter and a drone pipe.

78. Easter 1966 (song)

Unlike Nelson's Column in Trafalgar Square, Nelson's Pillar in Dublin had a troubled history. Many generations of Irish Republicans and nationalists deeply resented the pillar and its statue and showed their hatred by attempting to blow it up. After 157 years, the objective was finally achieved at 1.30 a.m. on 8 March 1966, the 50th Anniversary of the Easter Rising. The top half of the pillar was blown to smithereens in a dramatic explosion. The other half was carefully and ostentatiously demolished by the Irish Army. The fate of the stone head of Nelson is another story. There have been many popular Irish songs and poems written about the event. "The beauty that was born" is an allusion to the lines in W. B. Yeats' poem, "Easter, 1916": "All changed, changed utterly: / A terrible beauty is born."

THE WRITTEN WORD

81. A hermit in Vitsa

Vitsa is one of the Zagori villages, traditional settlements in Epirus, northwest Greece. Central Zagori. It is located above the Vikos Gorge, at an altitude of nearly 1000 metres. Wang Wei (*c.*700–*c.*760) was a Chinese Han poet and painter of the Tang Dynasty. Zhang Ji (*c.*715–*c.*780) was a Tang Dynasty poet, whose most famous poem is "Mooring at Night by Maple Bridge". My translation of that poem is included in *Reading the Signs* (London: Colenso Books, 2000, page 53). On Ryōkan see the note above to page 42 ("With Ryōkan . . .").

84. Skeletons of the past – a drunken man on Burns Night, 1959

This poem is an attempt to write pastiche Lallans (Lowland Scots dialect) in the style of MacDiarmid's own synthetic Scots; and "eternal lightning" is a reference to his poem 'The Skeleton of the Future (At Lenin's Tomb)":

> Red granite and black diorite, with the blue
> Of the labradorite crystals gleaming like precious stones
> In the light reflected from the snow; and behind them
> The eternal lightning of Lenin's bones.

Although I feel much closer to the poetry of Edwin Muir (see the note to pages 94–95 below) than to that of the prolific and equally important Hugh MacDiarmid, I often return to MacDiarmid's short Scots lyrics of 1923–1926 and to *A drunk man looks at the thistle*. I am less attracted by his long, rambling nationalist poems (although many can be challenging and stimulating), but I do value and engage with my two volumes of *The Complete Poems of Hugh MacDiarmid* and a first edition of *Lucky Poet: A Self Study in Literature and Political Ideas, Being the Autobiography of Hugh Macdiarmid* (1943). Hugh MacDiarmid was the nom-de-plume of Christopher Grieve, hence "Christopher, Chris or Hughie". MacDiarmid visited Prague in 1955 as a guest of the Spartakiad; and again in 1959, to give the Bicentennial Lecture celebrating the two hundredth anniversary of the birth of Robert Burns. He was as much interested in the beerhouses as he was in the political and the cultural life of Prague, according to one historian.

85. Byron haiku

The "Revolution" was the Greek War of Independence, on which see the note to page 92 below.

86. Enver Hoxha on Lord Byron
Hoxha, though holding many different official posts, was effectively the leader of communist Albania from WWII until his death in 1985. Although he rebuilt and developed a war-torn and backward country his regime became increasingly despotic and repressive and he kept Albania largely isolated from the rest of the world. On Byron's appreciation of Albania see the note to page 125 below.

86. Racedown, Dorset, September 1795 – June 1979
"Pinney's place", called Racedown Lodge, was where Wordsworth and his sister were invited to stay, rent-free, by his friend John Pinney, whose family owned large numbers of slaves on their sugar plantations on the island of Nevis in the West Indies. John's father was a prominent Bristol merchant and John himself was a member of the Bristol West Indies Trading Company. Pilsdon Pen is a prominent Iron Age hillfort in southwest Dorset where the Wordsworths liked to walk.

88–89. Big Sur to Bodega Bay
Henry Miller and Jack Kerouac both wrote books about Big Sur and. Miller lived there. *Koumbare* is the vocative of *koumbaros*, equivalent of "best man". In Greek culture the role involves a lifelong bond of mutual loyalty, a relationship not unlike that of a brother.

89. The Beats abroad
"The Hole" is US prison jargon which refers to the cramped and squalid solitary confinement cells in punishment cellblocks, as found in Carson section of Saint Quentin State Prison, California, but here used to imply a symbolic, generalised, nonspecific cell in any grim US prison.

91. 2103, the sky, maybe
Niki Marangou was a Cypriot poet, author and artist, actively involved in intercommunal bridge-building and peace initiatives on the island. She died in a car crash while travelling in Egypt in 2013.

92. One more spring
Nikiforos Vrettakos (1912–1991) was a prolific, optimistic and occasionally sentimental poet with a strong sense of *romiosyni*, on which see the note to page 69 ("In praise fo Bataria…) above. *Armatoli* were Christian Greeks employed by the Ottoman Turks as a body of military policemen, or a militia, to enforce law and order, to protect assigned districts from *klephts* and bandits. Later, during the Greek War of Independence (1821–1829), many changed sides and became guerrilla

fighters for the Greek cause. *Klephts* (from the Greek for "thieves") can be viewed as Greek brigands and bandits, or as freedom fighters during the Greek War of Independence. They had their haunts in the mountains, but they would come down to the valleys and act as highwaymen or kidnappers at various times. There are many Greek folk ballads about the heroic deeds of the *klephts*. Byron did much to raise awareness of the Greek cause in Britain and elsewhere in Europe and joined the Greek revolutionaries, dying of natural causes on the 19th of April 1824 in Missolonghi, where he had been involved in training troops. Many Greeks consider him as one the heroes of the War of Independence. In speaking of "the soldiers from his [Byron's] fatherland" and asking "what is it they've come here to do[...]?" Vrettakos was primarily referring to the events of December–January 1944 (already mentioned in the note to page 3 above). The German occupation had ended in October 1944, and on the 3rd of December Greek government forces and police had opened fire on a massive (200,000 strong) peaceful demonstration by left-wing resistance fighters and their associates against a British order for their immediate and unilateral disarmament. This action which left twenty-eight dead and many wounded, was the start of six weeks of armed conflict in the streets of Athens, in which British troops played an active part in the defeat of the left-wing fighters. The left had been promised, but were never given, a part in the post-liberation government. The Greek Civil War, which had started between the left-wing and right-wing resistance forces during WWII, now entered a new phase and continued until 1949.

93. Whatever Seferis says
The Greek poet and translator, Andreas Kalvos (1792–1869), once lived at 182 Sutherland Avenue, Maida Vale, London (now W9). Seferis' remarks were about Kalvos' time in Louth, but what he said about the damp and foggy atmosphere, draughty rooms and the smell of bacon and eggs apply equally to Maida Vale.

93. Joseph Jungmann's *Paradise Lost*
On Joseph Jungmann and Jungmannova Street, see the note below to page 96 ("Kafka and Steiner . . .").

94–95. November cloud
Professor Peter Butter (1921–1999) was the Regius Professor of English Language and Literature at the University of Glasgow. Edwin Muir (1887–1959) was a Scottish poet and translator who served as Director

of The British Institute in Prague 1945–1948. Both he and his wife Willa Muir wrote autobiographical accounts of their years in Prague. Dobříš Mansion (or Castle or Château) near Prague has a French garden and an English park; it was frequented by the *nomenklatura* — approved officials and members of the Union of Czech Writers during the Communist era; writers' conferences were held there. The Reich Protector (*Reichsprotektor*) held executive power in the Czech lands that were annexed by Nazi Germany, being known during WWII as the Protectorate of Bohemia and Moravia. Příbrám, southwest of Prague, in Central Bohemia, has a long mining history. "Dissidents' Mines" refers to dissidents and political prisoners who were opposed to the Communist regime and were sentenced to forced labour in the uranium mines. The historian František Bártík estimated that the death toll amongst those condemned to forced labour (from 1948 and throughout the 1950s) was around 500 men, as a result of accidents, suicides and possibly murders. There were others who died prematurely, after their release, because of the damage to their health from the harsh conditions and exposure to uranium. Paul Éluard (1895–1952) and Louis Aragon (1857–1982) were French Surrealist poets and both Communists. Willa Muir (1890–1970) was a Scottish novelist and translator (she and her husband Edwin Muir translated key works by Franz Kafka, among many other writers). Her autobiography, *Belonging: A Memoir* (1968) is a classic, and her hitherto unpublished novel, *The Usurpers*, set in Prague in the period from the late summer of 1945 to the end of July 1948, is due to be published by Colenso Books in 2022. "The Cloud" and "The Good Town" are poems of Edwin Muir's about his experiences in Prague around the time of the Communist putsch of 1948, as is "The Labyrinth", to which the last line alludes.

96. Kafka and Steiner, Prague, 28 March 1911

Franz Kafka (1883–1924) was employed for fourteen years by The Workmen's Accident Insurance Institute for the Kingdom of Bohemia. Although competent at his job, he was a man with many complexes, and was frustrated as it kept him from his writing. Rudolf Steiner (1861–1925) was an Austrian philosopher, involved for a time with the Theosophical Society before turning away to become an Anthroposophist. Jungmannova Street in central Prague has been home to many musical and cultural institutions. Josef Jungmann (1773–1847) was a Czech poet and linguist, a key figure in the Czech National Revival, and hugely influential in the development of the Czech language. His translation of Milton's *Paradise Lost* was an important building-block in the language of

NOTES

Czech literature. As the Count Lützow wrote (*Bohemian Literature*, revised edition, 1907), "It is really a wonderful achievement, if we consider that it was written in 1811, when the Bohemian language was only just awakening from its winter-sleep of nearly two hundred years."

96. Rilke at Duino, Joyce at Trieste

Rainer Maria Rilke (1875–1926) was a Bohemian–Austrian poet, born in Prague. He is one of the greatest and most influential of German-language poets. In 1911 he was a guest of Princess Maria von Thurn and Taxis-Hohenlohe at Duino Castle near Trieste; he started work on his first two *Duino Elegies* at the beginning of January 1912. The cycle of poems was not completed until February 1922. "Bloomtown" refers to the Dublin of Leopold Bloom the central character of James Joyce's novel *Ulysses* (1922). Ulysses or Odysseus is the hero of Homer's *Odyssey*, an account of Odysseus' multi-year voyage from the Trojan War back to his home in Ithaca and his adventures and misadventures on the way and after his arrival, while the novel follows Bloom's movements around Dublin in the course of a single day in 1904 — the 16th of June, celebrated since 1954 as Bloomsday.

98. In memory of Georgi Ivanov Markov

Markov was a dissident Bulgarian author who defected to London and worked for the BBC World Service and Radio Free Europe until he was murdered, probably by Bulgarian or Russian agents, in September 1978. Václav Havel (1936–2011) was a Czech playwright, essayist and former dissident, a founding member of Charter 77, who became President of Czechoslovakia after the Velvet Revolution of 1989. As for Saint Wite, very little is known about her. She is thought by some to have been a Saxon woman murdered by Viking raiders. In Whitchurch Canonicorum there is the church dedicated to Saint Candida and the Holy Cross, and inside the church is the shrine of Saint Candida. "Candida" is Latin for "white" and both Wite and Whit- in Whitchurch are variant forms of "white", all from Old English *hwīt*.

98. Yang's comparison

"Yang" is Yang Jiong, (seventh-century), a Chinese poet of the Tang Dynasty. The poem is related to one of Yang's in the genre of laments over the separation of friends, often civil servants (like Yang) posted to distant provinces.

99. To some British poets leaving Prague

TLS is *The Times Literary Supplement*. *Who's Who*, first published in 1949 and since 1996 available in an annually updated CD-ROM version is described by the publishers (Oxford University Press) as "the leading source of up-to-date information about over 35,000 influential people from all walks of life, worldwide. Containing autobiographical listings of people from around the globe who have an impact on British life, including senior politicians, judges, civil servants, and notable figures from the arts, academia, and other areas, it is seen as one of the world's most recognised and respected works of reference."

101. Auden and Dresden
A relevant further quotation from Auden comes from an interview by Michael Newman published as "W. H. Auden, The Art of Poetry No. 17" in *The Paris Review* 57 (Spring 1974): "I did a stint in the army, with the U.S. Strategic Bombing Survey. The army didn't like our report at all because we proved that, in spite of all our bombings of Germany, their weapons production didn't go down until after they had lost the war. It's the same in North Vietnam — the bombing does no good. But you know how army people are. They don't like to hear things that run contrary to what they've thought."

103. The Little Nobel
The expression "un-Eddic" relates to the poetic *Edda* — Old Norse or Icelandic alliterative minstrel poems. The Icelandic prose *Edda* of Snorri Sturluson (1179–1241) was compiled for young poets to learn how to praise kings of the Viking age, and records Norse legends and mythological tales of the Norse gods.

104. Sirmione, Lake Garda
Sirmione is a small town on the Sirmio promontory at the southern end of Lake Garda (the largest of Italy's lakes). The promontory is famous for its associations with the Latin poet Catullus (*c.*84–*c.*54 BC), renowned for his erotic poems, and the ruins of Roman villa, alleged to have been Catullus' country home. Lake Garda is described as "the Etruscan lake" because it lies within historic Etruria and the Etruscans first arrived in the area in the seventh century BC. "Lesbia" is the pseudonym Catullus gave to a lover who features in many of his poems.

FACING OFF THE THOUGHT POLICE

107. Thoughtcrimes
Winston Smith is the main character in George Orwell's dystopian novel,

1984, first published in 1949.

107. On a marble bust of Thomas Hardy
Sir Thomas Hamo Thornycroft (1850–1928) was an English sculptor and friend of Thomas Hardy, who sat for a portrait bust in marble (later cast in bronze) that was exhibited at the Royal Academy in 1916. "The Pity Of It" is a 1915 poem of Hardy's, a protest against warmongers, in which he emphasises the common ancestry, language and "kinship" of the people of Wessex and those of Saxon Germany, forced into conflict by sinister warlords. Hardy's poem "The Oxen", published in *The Times* on Christmas Eve 1915, is an agnostic's meditation on the Nativity which includes the line, "Come; see the oxen kneel".

108. Dampier's landfalls in New Holland
William Dampier (1651–1715), navigator, explorer and buccaneer from East Coker, Somerset was the first Englishman to explore parts of New Holland (Australia), which he visited on two occasions, in the *Cygnet* in 1688 and the *Roebuck* in 1699. On the first occasion he encountered the Bardi: "At our first coming, before we were acquainted with them, or they with us, a Company of them who liv'd on the Main, came just against our Ship, and standing on a pretty high Bank, threatened us with their Swords and Lances, by shaking them at us; at last the Captain ordered the Drum to be beaten, which was done of a sudden with much vigour, purposely to scare the poor Creatures. They hearing the noise, ran away as fast as they could drive, and when they ran away in haste, they would cry 'Gurry, Gurry', speaking deep in the Throat" (William Dampier, *A New Voyage Round the World*, London, 1697). It is generally accepted that "Gurry, Gurry" was an attempt to transcribe the word *ngaarri*, which meant a feared and malevolent spirit-being or devil. On the second voyage (1699) Dampier encountered the Djawi (Jawi) people. Dampier's men tried to capture a young man, but his companions reacted aggressively: "Upon seeing me, one of them threw a lance at me that narrowly missed me. I discharged my gun to scare them, but avoided shooting any of them; till finding the young man in danger from them, and myself in some, and that though the gun had a little frightened them at first, yet they had soon learnt to despise it, tossing up their hands and crying Pooh, Pooh, Pooh; and coming on afresh with a great noise, I thought it high time to charge again and shoot one of them, which I did" (Dampier, *A Voyage to New Holland, &c in the year, 1699*, London, 1703).

109. Wogganmagule
Sometimes written as "Woggan Ma Gule", it is an Aboriginal morning ceremony.

110. Red Hands Cave
The cave is in the Greenbrook area of the Blue Ridge Mountains National Park, about an hour's drive from Sydney. It was used for ceremonial purposes by the Darug people. The cave is famous for its impressive Aboriginal rock art — stencilled designs and hand prints in ochre, which are believed to be around 1,600 years old.

110. The dream came true — Captain Cook at Kealakekua Bay
Kealakekua Bay is located on the west coast of the main island of Hawaii, and marks the spot where Captain Sir James Cook was killed on the 14th of February, 1779, after relations with the Hawaiians had deteriorated as a result of mutual misunderstandings, following an initial welcome when the two ships (HMS *Resolution* and HMS *Discovery*) anchored on January 17th, 1779. It was at first believed that the god Orono or Lono had returned, as foretold in Hawaiian mythology. "Sandwich Islands" is the name that Cook gave to the Hawaiian archipelago.

112. Diamantina Roma and the postings of Governor Bowen
Sir George Bowen (1821–1899) had a thirty-year career in colonial government following an appointment in the Ionian Islands, where he served in Corfu as president of the Ionian Academy (1847–1851), before being made chief secretary to the government of the Ionian Islands. He was also an author. Later he was Governor successively of Queensland, New Zealand, Victoria, Mauritius, and Hong Kong. His Greek wife, Diamantina, Lady Bowen (née Contessa Diamantina di Roma, 1833–1893) is famous throughout Australia for her good works; they were married on Corfu in 1856. Her father was President of the Ionian Senate, and she was strongly attached to the island of Corfu. Maria Strani-Potts has written a paper on the challenging role of the accompanying spouse and on Diamantina's political influence in the Seven Islands and Australia, which was presented at the International Pan-Ionian Conference in 2004 (published, Corfu, 2018). "Men of the toga" refers to Oxbridge graduates and civil servants of the British Empire who could be easily satirised for their status- and rank-consciousness if they behaved arrogantly or took themselves too seriously, supposing themselves to be successors of the Roman *togati* and sticking together against outsiders to protect, project and consolidate their own powers

and privileges.

114. Imagined last words
Elijah Upjohn, originally from Shaftesbury in Dorset, was a convict in the Old Melbourne Gaol who volunteered (or was pressured) to act as hangman in the absence of the official executioner. This was his first execution. Ned Kelly (1854–1880) was an Australian bushranger and outlaw, famous in folklore and films, and the subject of a series of paintings by Sidney Nolan (see the note to page 116 below). Ned Kelly's *Jerilderie Letter*, written in Jerilderie in 1879, resembled a "republican manifesto" in which he attempted to justify his actions (he was a murderer and stock-thief). The poem is influenced by Ned's vivid style. Here's an excerpt from his defiant letter: "I have been wronged. And my mother and four or five men lagged innocent, and is my brothers and sisters and my mother not to be pitied also who was has [*sic.*] no alternative only to put up with the brutal and cowardly conduct of a parcel of big ugly, fat necked, wombat headed, big bellied, magpie legged, narrow hipped splaw-footed sons of Irish bailiffs or English landlords which is better known as officers of justice or Victorian police who some calls honest gentlemen."

114. Port Arthur — Isle of the Dead
Edward Spicer was one of the convicts transported to Van Diemen's Land (Tasmania) on the *Mayda* on the 27th of August 1845. The ship arrived on the 8th of January 1846. Henry Savery (1791–1842) was a convicted forger, sentenced to transportation to Van Diemen's Land. He was on board the *Medway*, which departed on the 25th of July 1825 and arrived at Van Diemen's Land on the 14th of December. He was Australia's first novelist, author of *Quintus Servinton: A Tale Founded upon Incidents of Real Occurrence*. After a period in Hobart, he was sentenced for further offences to imprisonment at the penal colony of Port Arthur. The Isle of the Dead is a small cemetery island close to Port Arthur

116. Reflecting, unreflecting
Sidney Nolan (1917–1992) produced a famous series of naïve-style Ned Kelly paintings, depicting aspects of the life of the legendary outlaw and his iconic body-armour. Sidney Nolan was knighted in 1981. He often worked with Ripolin and acrylic paints. "Queenie" is Queenie McKenzie (*c.*1915–1998), who was an outstanding East Kimberley Aboriginal artist. "Rover" is Rover Thomas (1926–1998), an equally inspiring East Kimberley Aboriginal artist. Both McKenzie and Thomas liked to paint

their subtle matt landscapes and their representations of Aboriginal creation myths and their environmental concerns using various shades of natural ochres.

116. Semiotics — Marrickville
Marrickville is a suburb of Sydney, New South Wales, a culturally diverse suburb populated in the past by many Greek immigrant families, later dominated by Vietnamese immigrants.

118. Pyrotechnics, November 5th
In Britain "the 5th of November", also known as "Bonfire Night" and "Guy Fawkes Night", is an occasion for bonfires and fireworks, on the date of a foiled plot of 1605 by Guy Fawkes and other Catholics to blow up the Houses of Parliament in London. Effigies, often straw-stuffed dummies, known as "Guys", are traditionally burned on the bonfires. The religious animosity once associated with this celebration is largely forgotten now, and this poem is about the pleasure and joy that firework displays can give, bringing people of all cultures and ages together — a poem about unity rather than division.

120. Sankt Göran och draken
The title is Swedish for "Saint George and the Dragon".

122. Paranoia, Risk för istappar!
The Swedish phrase in the title means "Risk of icicles!"

122. Paxos
On the location of island of Paxos, see the note to page 22 ("Paxiot fishermen").

123. The Igoumenos and the Saint
The Igoumenos is the Abbot of a Greek Orthodox monastery.

124. Acheiropoieta
This Greek word meaning "not made by hands" is used of holy icons believed to have been created miraculously without the use of human action.

124. On the need for a new Mission
From Thessaloniki, Cyril (born Constantine, 826–869), and his brother Methodius (815–885) evangelized the Slavs. Known as the "Apostles to the Slavs", they are credited with the invention of the Glagolitic alphabet, known in its later forms as "Cyrillic", used for Russian and a number of other Slavonic languages.

125. Land of Albania!

The title comes from Lord Byron's *Childe Harold's Pilgrimage* (II.8):
   Land of Albania! where Iskander rose,
   Theme of the young, and beacon of the wise,
   And he his namesake, whose oft-baffled foes
   Shrunk from his deeds of chivalrous emprize;
   Land of Albania! let me bend mine eyes
   On thee, thou rugged nurse of savage men!
   The cross descends, thy minarets arise,
   And the pale crescent sparkles in the glen,
   Through many a cypress grove within each city's ken.

Onufri was a famous sixteenth century icon painter. A muezzin is a man who calls faithful Muslims to prayer from the minaret of a mosque. Skenderbeg or Skanderbeg — also known as Gjergj Kastrioti, Iskander bej, George Castriot and Yorgos Kastriotis (1405–1468) — was an Albanian national hero and military commander of a league of Albanian princes, leader of the resistance to the expansion of the Ottoman Empire. In a sonnet by Edmund Spenser (*c*.1552–1599) he is called "the scourge of Turkes, and plague of infidels".

127. Neo Frourio, Kerkyra

The *Neo Frourio*, meaning "New Fortress", is the Venetian fortress in Corfu Town, built in the sixteenth and seventeenth centuries. Mount Pantocrator is the highest mountain (906m) on Corfu. The name is the equivalent of English "Almighty" but used as an epithet of Christ in majesty or Christ in judgement. The British were obliged by treaty to destroy the fortifications when the garrison withdrew after ceding the Ionian Islands to Greece in 1864. Vido Island, opposite Corfu Town, has played an important strategic role in the defence of Corfu throughout the centuries. The little island and the waters around it are held sacred by the Serbian people, because of the tragic events and deaths following the great evacuation to Corfu after the long march (exodus) of the defeated Serbian army in 1916. The ode *Plava grobnica* (*The Sea Grave*) by Milutin Bojić, dedicated to the dead soldiers, commemorates the 5,000 Serbian soldiers' deaths on the island and their sea burials, 1916–1918. Here is the first verse translated by Mihailo Djordjevic:
   Beneath the sea, on sleeping shells
   And weeds that gently fall,
   Lies a grave of heroes, brother next to brother,
   Prometheuses of hope, apostles of tragedy.

Lazaretto island, opposite Kontokali, served at various times as a leprosarium, Venetian quarantine station, military hospital, place of exile, and site of execution for between 112 and 120 political prisoners (Greek communists and resistance fighters), following incarceration in Corfu Prison and a night in the death cell, during and after the Greek Civil War; the great majority of executions took place between 1947 and 1949, though there was one as late as 1954.

127. Lazaretto
See the previous note. The ship *Achilleas* was used to transport the prisoners from Corfu to the island of execution, usually at dawn.

127. Along came Luccheni
Luigi Luccheni, (US spelling Lucheni, 1873–1910) was an Italian anarchist who assassinated Empress Elisabeth of Austria, stabbing her to death in Geneva on the 10th of September 1898.

128. Pylos
Pylos is a town on the western coast of the Peleponnese, once called Navarino and the site of a naval battle in 1827 which proved a decisive turning point in the Greek War of Independence. Codrington was in overall command of a joint British, French and Russian naval force which largely destroyed the Ottoman and Egyptian fleets. On Byron and the Greek War of Independence, see the note to page 92 above.

129. Welcome
On "December '44" see the note to page 92 above.

130. Nikolaides
This is not the schoolboy's real name. This poem was later translated into Greek by the Cypriot poet Niki Marangou, on whom see the note to page 91 ("2013, the sky, maybe") above.

131. Martial Law (marching song)
A satirical song about a military coup — anywhere. Greece under the Colonels and Ethiopia under the Derg (military junta) could have been at the back of my mind. A demo recording in an arrangement by Raul Scacchi can be found on YouTube (https://www.youtube.com/watch?v=HXpn_Fv3XZM).

132. Paidomazomo, Prague Airport, 1988
Paidomazomo alludes both to the Ottoman "blood tax" or "child levy" (*devşirme* or forced recruitment of Christian boys) and to the forced rounding-up (*mazoma*) and evacuation of Greek children (*paidia*) to

communist countries during the Greek Civil War. The reasons for the *paidomazomo* in 1948–1949 are contentious and subject to different ideological explanations.

132. Stavrula's father

On Metaxas see the note to page 72 above. Marshal Tito (1892–1980) was President of the Socialist Federal Republic of Yugoslavia from 1953 to 1980. Klement Gottwald (1896–1953) led the Czechoslovak Communist Party from 1929 to 1953. He was the hardline Chairman of the Party at the time that Stavrula's father arrived in Czechoslovakia. *Pare karpouzi, sintrofe* means "Have some watermelon, Comrade". Ostrava is an industrial and coalmining town, in the northeast of the Czech Republic. Many immigrants and political exiles worked there.

134. The Red Danube near Devín Castle, Bratislava

Devín Castle is in Slovakia at the confluence of the Danube and Morava rivers, on the frontier with Austria. Before 1989 it was a heavily-guarded military zone in what was then Czechoslovakia. People risked being shot if they attempted to escape by swimming across the river to the Austrian side. *Pozor!* means "Attention!"

136. First Impressions of Prague

Soon after I was posted to Czechoslovakia in April 1986, I wrote this, my first Prague poem. Antonín Dvořák (1841–1914) was Czechoslovakia's most famous composer. "Bloody apron" because his father was a butcher, and I'd read many times that Antonín Dvořák had been trained as an apprentice butcher, though more recently I learned that this was not the case. Yet his father *was* an innkeeper and butcher, like his predecessors, and young Antonín might well have worn a bloody apron on occasion, so the last line of the poem is not inaccurate, as he was expected to help with the family business, even if he didn't really learn the trade. He sometimes went to market with his father to choose the best livestock.

136. Right of way — "All in Bohemia's well"

"All in Bohemia's well" are words of Hermione to Leontes in Shakespeare's *The Winter's Tale* (Act 1, Scene 2). In this context, the word "Chartists" refers to those Czechoslovak dissidents who signed Charter 77; and "Jazzmen" refers to members of the persecuted Jazzová Sekce-Artforum (Jazz Section of the Musicians' Union). Members were persecuted for organizing concerts and exhibitions without approval and for publishing "unsuitable" literature. The organisation was banned during the 1980s and several of its members were imprisoned. Certain kinds of jazz music and musicians had already experienced a problematic history under the German Occupation. (See the influential novels of Josef Škvorecký, such as *The Bass Saxophone* and *The Cowards*, or his collection of essays *Talkin' Moscow Blues*.)

138. Karel Čapek and Mr Esquire
Dobrý večer means "Good evening" (with a sense of finality here), and *Tak teda sbohem* means "And so goodbye".

139. To the Czechs
On Cyril and Methodius, see the note to page 124 ("On the need for a new Mission") above. John Wycliffe (*c*.1320–1384), the English religious reformer, had a strong influence on Jan Hus (*c*.1372–1415), the Czech reformer. Peter Payne (*c*.1380–*c*.1455) was an English reformer and Taborite (a radical faction of the Hussites) who had escaped to Prague where he played a prominent role amongst the Czech reformers.

140. Jan Palach
Jan Palach (1948–1969) was a twenty-year-old Czech student at Charles University, Prague, who set himself on fire as a protest against the 1968 invasion by the Warsaw Pact armies. The end of the Prague Spring and his death from an act of self-immolation had profound international repercussions.

140. Václav Havel's Trial
Havel, the playwright and dissident who would be elected President by the end of the year (29th of December 1989), after the Velvet Revolution, was sentenced at this trial for inciting illegal protests (e.g. to commemorate Jan Palach's ultimate sacrifice) and for obstructing the police. The vindictive sentence was nine months in prison.

141. Black Sea — decomposition — searching for loved ones
Baltermants (1912–1990) was born in Poland but became a famous Soviet war photographer. His photographs of the aftermath of the Nazi death-squad massacres of the Jews of Kerch produced unforgettable and deeply shocking images (initially censored) of the grieving village women searching for their loved ones. Atlas Gallery later commented, "A powerful oversaturated sky above, burnt in during the printing of the photo, makes the image even more dramatic." It seems strange that such an overpowering image as "Grief" was subjected to considerations of dramatic heightening or artistic composition.

NOTES

142. On the Silesian Express to Warsaw

Theresienstadt is the German name of a fortress and garrison town in Bohemia, which became the site of an infamous concentration camp and ghetto for Jews during WWII. Terezín is the Czech name. Lidice is remembered around the world for the horrific reprisal massacre, in June 1942, of all the male population of the village over fifteen years of age.

143. Arbeit macht frei

Arbeit macht frei ("Work makes [one] free") was the sign over the entrances to Terezín, Auschwitz and other concentration camps. Grandfather Čech was the legendary founder of the Czech nation. Říp is the Bohemian mountain where the first Czechs are thought to have arrived. On Terezín, see the previous note.

143. Last Christmas in Prague — Kaprová Koleda

Kaprová Koleda means "Carp Carol" (kaprová is my made-up word). Carp (*kapr*) is the traditional Czech Christmas meal. *Veselme se? Radujme se?* means "Let's all be merry? Let's all rejoice?" Note the ironical question marks (suggesting this is not likely in such a repressive political situation) inserted after these phrases from a traditional (fifteenth-century) Czech Christmas carol:

> *Narodil se Kristus Pán, veselme se,*
> *z růže kvítek vykvet' nám, radujme se!*
> *He was born Christ the Lord, let's all be merry,*
> *This flower bloomed from the rose, let us rejoice.*

Ryba is the Czech for "fish", but here intended to evoke the name of Jakub Jan Ryba (1765–1815), composer of the popular Christmas folk-mass or *Czech Christmas Mass* (1796); "a dying fall of Ryba" because the carp is kept in the bath before being killed for Christmas, and Ryba, the composer of such happy music, committed suicide.

144. Persons of Interest

770,000 names can be found in the StB database. The list was based on the Register of Persons of Interest (EZO), a basic component of the extensive information system of the StB. The inclusion of a person's name was said to indicate nothing more than that the StB was interested in that person; that he or she, whether a national or a foreigner, was someone they felt needed to be watched, just in case. A "blocked person" on the register (Blokovaná Osoba) was possibly blocked to avoid complications when the various police forces and sections of the secret police were interested in the same person.

Lightning Source UK Ltd.
Milton Keynes UK
UKHW012151251121
394574UK00001B/46